GW00675831

Notting Hill Editions is an independent British Publisher devoted to restoring the art of the essay. The company was founded by Tom Kremer, champion of innovation and the man responsible for popularising the Rubik's Cube.

After a successful career in toy invention, Tom decided, at the age of eighty, to engage his life-long passion for the essay. In a digital world, where time is short and books are cheap, he judged the moment was right to launch a counter-culture. He founded Notting Hill Editions with a mission: to restore this largely neglected art as a cornerstone of literary culture, and to produce beautiful books that would not be thrown away.

The unique purpose of the essay is to try out ideas and see where they lead. Hailed as 'the shape of things to come', we aim to publish books that shift perspectives, prompt argument, make imaginative leaps, and reveal truth.

William Makepeace Thackeray (1811–1863) was born in India before coming to England for a public school and Cambridge University education. He wanted to be an artist but had better luck with the pen. After ten years of jobbing work his first great success was *Vanity Fair* in 1847. Despite ill health, he continued writing monthly serials which established him as Dickens's nearest rival. He died prematurely in his early fifties.

John Sutherland is the Lord Northcliffe Professor Emeritus at UCL. He has been a devoted reader and critic of Thackeray ever since his tutor, Monica Jones, encouraged him to read *Vanity Fair*. His first book was *Thackeray at Work*, a study of Thackeray's wonderfully casual creativity. John Sutherland has edited the author's three major works *Vanity Fair*, *Pendennis*, and *Esmond*, as well as his most bitingly satirical minor work, *The Snobs of England*.

Published in 2018
by Notting Hill Editions Ltd
Widworthy Barton Honiton Devon EX14 9JS

Designed by FLOK Design, Berlin, Germany
Typeset by CB editions, London

Template cover design by FLOK Design, Berlin, Germany
Cover design by Plain Creative, UK

Printed and bound
by Memminger MedienCentrum, Memmingen, Germany

Introduction and notes copyright © 2018 by John Sutherland

All rights reserved

The right of John Sutherland to be identified as the author
of the Introduction to this work has been asserted in accordance
with Section 77 of the Copyright, Designs and Patents Act 1998

This book is sold subject to the condition that it shall not, by way of
trade or otherwise, be lent, resold, hired out or otherwise circulated
without the publisher's prior consent in any form of binding or cover
other than that in which it is published and without a similar condition
including this condition being imposed on the subsequent purchaser.

A CIP record for this book
is available from the British Library

ISBN 978-1-910749-92-0

www.nottinghilleditions.com

Samuel Laurence: Portrait of Thackeray in Middle Age

A ROUNDABOUT MANNER

Sketches of Life by W. M. Thackeray

–

introduced by
John Sutherland

Notting Hill Editions

Contents

– ILLUSTRATIONS –

John Sutherland

– Introduction –

I was inducted into a lifetime love of Thackeray by a remarkable woman: Monica Jones, a lecturer at Leicester University, is known nowadays as the paramour and muse of Philip Larkin.

Jones's views on life and literature, which she studiously refrained from putting into print (most academic publication was, she believed, drivel) permeated the work of Britain's most esteemed twentieth-century poet. They also had a formative effect on lesser me.

It was Miss Jones who directed me, tutorially, to Thackeray with the instruction: 'He will be gold in your pocket for life.' He could jingle there alongside her other two favourite authors, George Crabbe and Walter Scott.

I went on to do a doctoral thesis on Thackeray and a book on his uniquely relaxed working methods. Fuelled by my fascination with him, I later edited the three major novels: *Vanity Fair*, *Pendennis*, and *Henry Esmond*, digging into the dust that, alas, lies thicker on their author than it does on Dickens, the Brontës, George Eliot, or even the 'lesser Thackeray', Anthony Trollope.

My aim was simple –I wanted to get as close to the

man as a century's historical distance would allow. As part of that project I spent hours contemplating the Queen Anne House he designed and built for himself – 2 Palace Green, Kensington. It is now the Israeli embassy.

Thackeray's house in Palace Green, Kensington

The house embodies in red bricks his Augustan view of life, but the hem of the robe for me was the manuscripts: one touches what his hand and pen touched. Thackeray's literary remains are *disjecta membra*, torn into posthumous fragments and scattered in scores of repositories by nineteenth-century admirers and souvenir hunters. I felt, glamorously, like a scholar-adventurer hunting them down – an unusual feeling in academic life.

These literary remains, as their crests and

occasional stains often testify, were written of an evening in one of his clubs (prominently the Garrick, Reform, and Athenaeum), the author creatively 'warmed' with wine (he loved the 'cloop' of the bottle's opening and had a famously refined palate). The printer's boy waited eagerly for the sheets next morning outside his house door. Unlike Dickens, whose script is tangled, Thackeray's handwriting style was legible and slipped effortlessly into print.

That clubman easygoingness is the essence of Thackeray. It breathes over all his published work. He will never, like Austen, Dickens or Brontë, embellish a British banknote or postage stamp – but he has a fine memorial room at the Reform Club ornamented with a magnificent portrait of him by Samuel Laurence.

At the very end of his life he was advised by his doctors to exercise. In his diary he recorded his daily exertion as the number of steps he took (foreswearing the cab) from his house to the Athenaeum, where, doubtless, he undid his good pedestrian work with a hearty lunch. In his club, with fellow members of a like mind, Thackeray was free to converse. The Thackerayan voice itself, as recalled by friends, was metropolitan, a little high-pitched (he was not a good lecturer), occasionally man-among-men bawdy, always witty, and tinged with world-weary melancholy.

One *sees* Dickens, in what critics have called the 'Dickens Theatre'. But one *hears* that unmistakable Thackerayan voice in everything Thackeray wrote. He converses with us. Take, for instance, the famous *envoi* to *Vanity Fair*:

Ah! Vanitas Vanitatum! Which of us is happy in this world? Which of us has his desire? or, having it, is satisfied? – Come, children, let us shut up the box and the puppets, for our play is played out.

The children are Thackeray's daughters

Thackeray's life was cut short but he left us millions of words. Over half of them are 'casual', occasional, journalistic – above all, essayistic. What was it Samuel Johnson called the essay? 'A loose sally of the mind.' That description, the unloosed sallying mind, fits Thackeray's *oeuvre* perfectly.

Thackeray's 'stock' was Yorkshire gentry – he had, his biographer Gordon N. Ray reminds us, the three generations behind him which make an English gentleman. As Ray also argues, Thackeray's great endeavour in his writing was to redefine traditional English ideals of what it was to be a gentleman, historically the exclusive property of aristocracy and royalty – for the emergent middle classes of Victorian England. The new genus of gentleman could be noble, whether his blood were blue or not. The finest gentleman in *Vanity Fair* is William Dobbin, whose father was a greengrocer.

William Makepeace Thackeray was born in 1811 in India – a country which, after the age of seven, he never revisited but which haunted him throughout life. William's father was a senior colonial administrator before dying prematurely in 1816 – leaving, in addition to his only legitimate child, a daughter by his Indian concubine. Thackeray was never entirely stable on the subject of race (particularly Indians); nor did he ever publicly acknowledge the existence of his half-sister Sarah.

His mother remarried. She had, before she married Thackeray's father, loved another. The family resolved he was 'inappropriate' and misinformed her he had died. Something more appropriate was arranged. It was a cruel trick, but a not unknown practice among her class, for whom class was everything. After the death of her husband, Thackeray's father, she discovered the existence of this supposedly dead first love. He became her second husband.

Thackeray never knew his father but loved his stepfather, and immortalised the old gentleman as his Quixote *de nos jours*, Colonel Newcome, in *The Newcomes* (serialised 1853–5). His evangelically severe mother he was never quite sure about. She is depicted as the morally stern Mrs Pendennis, in his second full-length serial. The depiction did not amuse her.

Infant William was returned to England, aged seven, to receive the education of a gentleman at Charterhouse and Trinity College, Cambridge. On the way back, the ship touched at St Helena, where he caught a glimpse of Napoleon – sowing the seed of a lifetime fascination with the Napoleonic Wars. The seed would bloom into *Vanity Fair*.

An idler at school, Thackeray left Cambridge a most undistinguished graduate, having lost much of his sizeable patrimony gambling. On the way down, he picked up venereal disease, which hastened his death and caused him lifelong urethral difficulties. (On being introduced to a Mr Peawell in later years, he sighed 'I wish I could.') On the plus side, his early errors supplied the raw material for his fine *Bildungsroman* (self-portrait novel), *The History of Pendennis* (1850). Novelists waste nothing – not even their own wastefulness.

After false starts in law in England, and drawing and journalism in Paris, the prodigiously gifted but wayward young man embarked on a ten-year-long stint, 'writing for his life' with anonymous or pseud-onymous 'magazinery'. He wrote under a mass of *noms de plume*, around thirty in all, belonging to invented characters from all walks of life.

A roll call of 'the other Thackerays' would include Michel Angelo Titmarsh, OFC (Our Fat Correspond-ent), Mr Snob, Mr Roundabout, Yellowplush (a flun-key, with an uncertain grasp of orthography), and his comrade of the servant world C. Jeames de la Pluche, George Savage Fitz-Boodle, Esq, and Major Goliah Gahagan. It was an apprenticeship but, at the standard penny-a-line, a tough one. He could have gone under at any point.

By 1836 he had squandered what remained of his personal fortune and had improvidently married an Irish girl with no dowry. Having borne him two daughters, poor Isabella fell into incurable insan-ity and was discreetly put away. Thackeray could now never marry – unless, as Mr Rochester intends in *Jane Eyre*, bigamously. When Charlotte Brontë's novel came out there was absurd gossip that she and Thackeray were indeed clandestine lovers. It did not damage their sales.

By the early 1840s, Thackeray had made a reputa-tion for himself as a savagely cynical satirist. He had his first unequivocal success as a writer with *The Snobs of England* (1846–7), published in the congenial columns of the newly launched magazine *Punch*.

At the same time that the snob papers were

enlarging *Punch*'s sales by 5,000 copies a week, Thackeray was nursing a more ambitious narrative, something he initially called 'A Novel without a Hero'. Eventually *Vanity Fair*, as it was brilliantly renamed, came out in Dickensian monthly instalments, at one shilling, 32-page parts, illustrated by the novelist himself. He was, at this breakthrough moment in his career, some thirty-five years old and had published millions of words, but this was the first work to proclaim the name William Makepeace Thackeray to the world. He was a penny-a-liner no more.

Success mellows a man, and Thackeray's world view was markedly less cynical after *Vanity Fair*. It also accompanied important changes in his domestic arrangements: he set up home in Kensington with his daughters and – while remaining a clubman – was also a paterfamilias and less the bohemian. Thackeray had a number of grand projects as a writer once fame had come his way. Prominent among them was a desire to raise what he called 'the dignity of literature': to make it a gentlemanly occupation. No more Grub Street. It brought him into conflict with the supremely great novelist of the time, Dickens, whose early years gave him a better acquaintance with Marshalsea debtors' prison (where his father was confined) than Trinity College Cambridge.

Most discriminating Victorian readers would have agreed that these two were the supreme male novelists of the mid-century. Some partisans would have gone so far as to agree with Jane Carlyle (Thomas Carlyle's wife) that Thackeray 'beats Dickens out of the world'. The truth is that Dickens, even in their lifetimes, outsold Thackeray by as much as five to one. But Thackeray got a more thoughtful respect from the critics than Dickens. John Gibson Lockhart (Walter Scott's son-in-law), for example, dismissed *Pickwick* as 'all very well, but damned *low*'. Personal criticism and insult were levelled at Thackeray in his lifetime (e.g. that in his later years he was a 'mountain of blubber'). But no-one ever accused him, or his works, of being 'low'.

The writers were polite about and to each other. And sometimes more. Dickens actually saved Thackeray's life in 1849, when his rival succumbed to the cholera epidemic sweeping through London. Dickens sent his friend John Elliotson, the best doctor in London, to treat Thackeray. He dedicated his interrupted serial in progress, *Pendennis*, to Elliotson ('I never should have risen, but for your constant watchfulness and skill'). Indirectly it was Dickens he was thanking.

Thackeray published his most 'careful' novel, the 'three-decker' *History of Henry Esmond* in 1852. The narrative – loosely modelled on Scott's *Waverley* – is set in Thackeray's beloved Queen Anne period. Like Thomas Macaulay and other proponents of the Whig thesis,[1] Thackeray saw the early eighteenth century as

1. Bluntly that the wellbeing of England could be entrusted to well-meaning leaders of an otherwise Tory disposition. It was refined in Disraeli's 'One Nation' Toryism.

the moment when British parliamentary democracy, and its middle-class hegemony, came into being. No guillotines required on this side of the Channel.

Thackeray's career, in the tragically few years which remained to him, was glorious but none of his subsequent full-length fictions (*The Newcomes*, *The Virginians*, *The Adventures of Philip*) attained his earlier brilliance. But as editor of the newly launched *Cornhill Magazine*, with the highest-ever stipend of his career, Thackeray created his last great pen name, Mr Roundabout. This 'chronicler of small beer' (as Thackeray called him), was arguably his supreme literary creation. No Victorian 'prosed' better, or in more voices, than William Makepeace Thackeray.

He did not live to enjoy his Kensington mansion, dying prematurely in 1863, aged fifty-two. The postmortem revealed that his brain was preternaturally large: something that surprises no one who reads his fiction.

Dickens delivered, a week or so after Thackeray's death, a bittersweet obituary comment in the *Cornhill*:

We had our differences of opinion. I thought that he too much feigned a want of earnestness, and that he made a pretence of under-valuing his art, which was not good for the art that he held in trust. But, when we fell upon these topics, it was never very gravely, and I have a lively image of him in my mind, twisting both his hands in his hair, and stamping about, laughing, to make an end of the discussion.

Rivalry? Yes. But respect as well. Their writing careers had indeed been a kind of contest. But blessed the era which can boast two such writers as Charles Dickens and William Makepeace Thackeray.

———

What, though, underlay the prolific Thackerayan masquerade? Schopenhauer, that kindred spirit, notes the odd fact that *person* (what we really are) and *personae* ('masks' to disguise our real selves), are, at root, the same word. As T. S. Eliot puts it, our daily endeavour is to 'prepare a face to meet the faces that you meet'.

Thackeray plays with the idea of his other selves in the tailpiece to Chapter 8 of *Vanity Fair*, in which he has come down to talk to the reader in propria persona, 'in person' (but has he?):

Thackeray's ironic self-portrait in *Vanity Fair*

It is Thackeray, of course, as a confused little boy, wondering who on earth he is.

I began by recalling that my Thackerayan mission, once set on my way by Miss Jones, was to come close to the man himself. Did I strip off the last mask to find what lay beneath? No. Can anyone? No. Thackeray expressed the impossibility of our really knowing anyone else in one of his meditative asides in *Pendennis*:

How lonely we are in the world; how selfish and secret, everybody! . . . you and I are but a pair of infinite isolations, with some fellow-islands a little more or less near to us.

– NOTE TO READER –

The samples of Thackerayana in the following pages are arranged chronologically, and comprise essays, articles, extracts from longer works, and cartoons – a feast of many dishes.

None of them, I think it is safe to say, can be fully understood without some foreknowledge of the circumstances in which they were produced; nor without some brief explanation of references which his contemporaries picked up but will be elusive to the modern reader.

– A Gambler's Death –

Signed 'M. A. Titmarsh' – from *The Paris Sketch Book* (1840)

Before photography established itself, the 'sketch' with pen or pencil was the way of freezing the fleeting moment. In a sense all Thackeray's writing could carry the subtitle he gave Vanity Fair *– 'Pen and Pencil Sketches of English Society'.*

The Paris Sketch Book *was Thackeray's first full-length publication. The title is misleading. It is a compendium of occasional writings. Some, like 'A Gambler's Death', were gathered under the pseudonym Michael Angelo Titmarsh.*

In this tale, Thackeray draws on his own experience of Charterhouse, a public school. 'The story is, for the chief part, a fact,' he asserts in a footnote.

Jack Attwood, Titmarsh's old schoolfriend from Charterhouse, is a military hero ruined by drink and gambling. This, Thackeray feared, could be his own destiny. His biographer Gordon Ray notes, 'until he lost his fortune, Thackeray was totally unable to overcome his compulsion to gamble'. He was, moreover, what card sharpers called a 'gull', or 'pigeon', easily separated from his money.

The Paris Sketch Book *is dedicated, rather quaintly, to a French tailor who loaned the author a thousand francs when he was hard up. That money could well have gone on the casino tables.*

Anybody who was at C— school[1] some twelve years since, must recollect Jack Attwood: he was the most dashing lad in the place, with more money in his pocket than belonged to the whole fifth form in which we were companions.

When he was about fifteen, Jack suddenly retreated from C—, and presently we heard that he had a commission in a cavalry regiment,[2] and was to have a great fortune from his father, when that old gentleman should die. Jack himself came to confirm these stories a few months after, and paid a visit to his old school chums. He had laid aside his little school-jacket and inky corduroys, and now appeared in such a splendid military suit as won the respect of all of us. His hair was dripping with oil, his hands were covered with rings, he had a dusky down over his upper lip which looked not unlike a moustache, and a multiplicity of frogs and braiding on his surtout[3] which would have sufficed to lace a field-marshal. When old Swishtail, the usher, passed in his seedy black coat and gaiters, Jack gave him such a look of contempt as set us all a-laughing: in fact it was his turn to laugh now; for he used to roar very stoutly some months before, when Swishtail was in the custom of belabouring him with his great cane.[4]

1. Charterhouse.
2. Until the 1870s, commissions (i.e. officer-class rank) had to be bought in the English army.
3. Greatcoat.
4. Ushers were junior, or lower-grade teachers. They could not flog upper class boys – that was the privilege of the masters.

Jack's talk was all about the regiment and the fine fellows in it: how he had ridden a steeple-chase with Captain Boldero, and licked him at the last hedge; and how he had very nearly fought a duel with Sir George Grig, about dancing with Lady Mary Slamken at a ball. 'I soon made the baronet know what it was to deal with a man of the n—th,' said Jack. 'Dammee, sir, when I lugged out my barkers,[5] and talked of fighting across the mess-room table, Grig turned as pale as a sheet, or as –'

'Or as you used to do, Attwood, when Swishtail hauled you up,' piped out little Hicks, the foundation-boy.[6]

It was beneath Jack's dignity to thrash anybody, now, but a grown-up baronet; so he let off little Hicks, and passed over the general titter which was raised at his expense. However, he entertained us with his histories about lords and ladies, and so-and-so 'of ours', until we thought him one of the greatest men in his Majesty's service, and until the school-bell rung; when, with a heavy heart, we got our books together, and marched in to be whacked by old Swishtail. I promise you he revenged himself on us for Jack's contempt of him. I got that day at least twenty cuts to my share, which ought to have belonged to Cornet

5. Pistols. Duelling was abolished in the 1840s, largely under the initiative of Prince Albert.
6. i.e., attending Charterhouse on reduced fees, by virtue of passing a foundation examination.

Attwood, of the n—th dragoons.

When we came to think more coolly over our quondam[7] schoolfellow's swaggering talk and manner, we were not quite so impressed by his merits as at his first appearance among us. We recollected how he used, in former times, to tell us great stories, which were so monstrously improbable that the smallest boy in the school would scout them; how often we caught him tripping in facts, and how unblushingly he admitted his little errors in the score of veracity. He and I, though never great friends, had been close companions: I was Jack's form-fellow (we fought with amazing emulation for the *last* place in the class); but still I was rather hurt at the coolness of my old comrade, who had forgotten all our former intimacy, in his steeple-chases with Captain Boldero and his duel with Sir George Grig.

Nothing more was heard of Attwood for some years; a tailor one day came down to C—, who had made clothes for Jack in his school-days, and furnished him with regimentals: he produced a long bill for one hundred and twenty pounds and upwards, and asked where news might be had of his customer. Jack was in India, with his regiment, shooting tigers and jackals, no doubt. Occasionally, from that distant country, some magnificent rumour would reach us of his proceedings. Once I heard that he had been called to a court-martial for unbecoming conduct; another time,

7. 'One-time'.

that he kept twenty horses, and won the gold plate at the Calcutta races. Presently, however, as the recollections of the fifth form wore away, Jack's image disappeared likewise, and I ceased to ask or think about my college[8] chum.

A year since, as I was smoking my cigar in the 'Estaminet du Grand Balcon',[9] an excellent smoking-shop, where the tobacco is unexceptionable, and the Hollands[10] of singular merit, a dark-looking, thick-set man, in a greasy well-cut coat, with a shabby hat, cocked on one side of his dirty face, took the place opposite me, at the little marble table, and called for brandy. I did not much admire the impudence or the appearance of my friend, nor the fixed stare with which he chose to examine me. At last, he thrust a great greasy hand across the table, and said, 'Titmarsh, do you forget your old friend Attwood?'

I confess my recognition of him was not so joyful as on the day ten years earlier, when he had come, bedizened with lace and gold rings, to see us at C— school: a man in the tenth part of a century learns a deal of worldly wisdom, and his hand, which goes naturally forward to seize the gloved finger of a millionnaire, or a milor, draws instinctively back from a dirty fist, encompassed by a ragged wristband and a tattered cuff. But Attwood was in nowise so backward;

8. Charterhouse school referred to itself as a 'college'.
9. Drinking shop with a large balcony on which to smoke.
10. Gin.

and the iron squeeze with which he shook my passive paw, proved that he was either very affectionate or very poor. You, my dear sir, who are reading this history, know very well the great art of shaking hands: recollect how you shook Lord Dash's hand the other day, and how you shook *off* poor Blank, when he came to borrow five pounds of you.

However, the genial influence of the Hollands speedily dissipated anything like coolness between us and, in the course of an hour's conversation, we became almost as intimate as when we were suffering together under the ferule[11] of old Swishtail. Jack told me that he had quitted the army in disgust; and that his father, who was to leave him a fortune, had died ten thousand pounds in debt: he did not touch upon his own circumstances; but I could read them in his elbows, which were peeping through his old frock.[12] He talked a great deal, however, of runs of luck, good and bad; and related to me an infallible plan for breaking all the play-banks in Europe – a great number of old tricks; – and a vast quantity of gin-punch was consumed on the occasion; so long, in fact, did our conversation continue, that, I confess it with shame, the sentiment, or something stronger, quite got the better of me, and I have, to this day, no sort of notion how our palaver concluded. – Only, on the next morning, I did not possess a certain five-pound note which on

11. Iron-ringed cane.
12. Frock coat.

the previous evening was in my sketch-book (by far the prettiest drawing by the way in the collection) but there, instead, was a strip of paper, thus inscribed: –

I. O. U.
Five Pounds. JOHN ATTWOOD,
Late of the N—th Dragoons.

I suppose Attwood borrowed the money, from this remarkable and ceremonious acknowledgment on his part: had I been sober I would just as soon have lent him the nose on my face; for, in my then circumstances, the note was of much more consequence to me.

As I lay, cursing my ill fortune, and thinking how on earth I should manage to subsist for the next two months, Attwood burst into my little garret – his face strangely flushed – singing and shouting as if it had been the night before. 'Titmarsh', cried he, 'you are my preserver! – my best friend! Look here, and here, and here!' And at every word Mr Attwood produced a handful of gold, or a glittering heap of five-franc pieces, or a bundle of greasy, dusky bank-notes, more beautiful than either silver or gold: – he had won thirteen thousand francs after leaving me at midnight in my garret. He separated my poor little all, of six pieces, from this shining and imposing collection; and the passion of envy entered my soul: I felt far more anxious now than before, although starvation was then staring me in the face; I hated Attwood for *cheating* me out of all this wealth. Poor fellow! it had been better for him had he never seen a shilling of it.

However, a grand breakfast at the Café Anglais dissipated my chagrin; and I will do my friend the justice to say, that he nobly shared some portion of his good fortune with me. As far as the creature comforts were concerned I feasted as well as he, and never was particular as to settling my share of the reckoning.

Jack now changed his lodgings; had cards, with Captain Attwood engraved on them, and drove about a prancing cab-horse, as tall as the giraffe at the Jardin des Plantes;[13] he had as many frogs[14] on his coat as in the old days, and frequented all the flash restaurateurs' and boarding-houses of the capital. Madame de Saint Laurent, and Madame la Baronne de Vaudrey, and Madame la Comtesse de Jonville, ladies of the highest rank, who keep a *société choisie* and condescend to give dinners at five-francs a head, vied with each other in their attentions to Jack. His was the wing of the fowl, and the largest portion of the Charlotte-Russe; his was the place at the écarté table, where the Countess would ease him nightly of a few pieces, declaring that he was the most charming cavalier, la fleur d'Albion. Jack's society, it may be seen, was not very select; nor, in truth, were his inclinations: he was a careless, dare-

13. Paris's botanical gardens had, at this period, a menagerie, or zoo attached to it.
14. Frogs – ornamental braid.

devil, Macheath[15] kind of fellow, who might be seen daily with a wife on each arm.

It may be supposed that, with the life he led, his five hundred pounds of winnings would not last him long; nor did they; but, for some time, his luck never deserted him; and his cash, instead of growing lower, seemed always to maintain a certain level: he played every night.

Of course, such a humble fellow as I, could not hope for a continued acquaintance and intimacy with Attwood. He grew overbearing and cool, I thought; at any rate I did not admire my situation as his follower and dependant, and left his grand dinner for a certain ordinary, where I could partake of five capital dishes for ninepence. Occasionally, however, Attwood favored me with a visit, or gave me a drive behind his great cab-horse. He had formed a whole host of friends besides. There was Fips, the barrister; heaven knows what he was doing at Paris; and Gortz, the West Indian,[16] who was there on the same business, and Flapper, a medical student, – all these three I met one night at Flapper's rooms, where Jack was invited, and a great 'spread' was laid in honour of him.

Jack arrived rather late – he looked pale and agitated; and, though he ate no supper, he drank raw brandy

15. The highwayman hero of John Gay's *The Beggar's Opera* (1728).
16. i.e., mixed race, from a parent enriched by the sugar trade, like the Jewish-Jamaican Miss Swartz in *Vanity Fair*.

in such a manner as made Flapper's eyes wink: the poor fellow had but three bottles, and Jack bade fair to swallow them all. However, the West Indian generously remedied the evil, and producing a napoleon, we speedily got the change for it in the shape of four bottles of champagne.

Our supper was uproariously harmonious; Fips sung the good 'Old English Gentleman'; Jack the 'British Grenadiers'; and your humble servant, when called upon, sang that beautiful ditty, 'When the Bloom is on the Rye',[17] in a manner that drew tears from every eye, except Flapper's, who was asleep, and Jack's, who was singing the 'Bay of Biscay O', at the same time. Gortz and Fips were all the time lunging at each other with a pair of single-sticks, the barrister having a very strong notion that he was Richard the Third.

At last Fips hit the West Indian such a blow across his sconce, that the other grew furious; he seized a champagne-bottle, which was, providentially, empty, and hurled it across the room at Fips: had that celebrated barrister not bowed his head at the moment, the Queen's Bench would have lost one of its most eloquent practitioners.

Fips stood as straight as he could; his cheek was pale with wrath. 'M-m-ister Go-gortz,' he said, 'I always heard you were a blackguard; now I can pr-pr-

17. An actual ballad. A favourite item in James Joyce's after-dinner repertoire.

peperove it. Flapper, your pistols! every ge-ge-genlmn knows what I mean.'

Young Mr Flapper had a small pair of pocket-pistols, which the tipsy barrister had suddenly remembered, and with which he proposed to sacrifice the West Indian. Gortz was nothing loth, but was quite as valorous as the lawyer.

Attwood, who, in spite of his potations, seemed the soberest man of the party, had much enjoyed the scene, until this sudden demand for the weapons. 'Pshaw!' said he, eagerly, 'don't give these men the means of murdering each other; sit down and let us have another song.'

But they would not be still; and Flapper forthwith produced his pistol-case, and opened it, in order that the duel might take place on the spot. There were no pistols there! 'I beg your pardon,' said Attwood, looking much confused; 'I – I took the pistols home with me to clean them!'

I don't know what there was in his tone, or in the words, but we were sobered all of a sudden. Attwood was conscious of the singular effect produced by him, for he blushed, and endeavoured to speak of other things, but we could not bring our spirits back to the mark again, and soon separated for the night. As we issued into the street, Jack took me aside, and whispered, 'Have you a napoleon,[18] Titmarsh, in your

18. Twenty-franc gold coin, equivalent to the English Sovereign.

purse?' Alas! I was not so rich. My reply was, that I was coming to Jack, only in the morning, to borrow a similar sum.

He did not make any reply, but turned away homeward: I never heard him speak another word.

—

Two mornings after (for none of our party met on the day succeeding the supper), I was awakened by my porter, who brought a pressing letter from Mr Gortz.

> DEAR T. –
> 'I wish you would come over here to breakfast.
> There's a row about Attwood.
> 'Yours truly,
> SOLOMON GORTZ.'

I immediately set forward to Gortz's; he lived in the Rue du Helder, a few doors from Attwood's new lodging. If the reader is curious to know the house in which the catastrophe of this history took place, he has but to march some twenty doors down from the Boulevard des Italiens, when he will see a fine door, with a naked Cupid shooting at him from the hall, and a Venus beckoning him up the stairs.

On arriving at the West Indian's, at about mid-day (it was a Sunday morning), I found that gentleman in his dressing-gown, discussing, in the company of Mr Fips, a large plate of *bifteck aux pommes*.

'Here's a pretty row!' said Gortz, quoting from his letter; – 'Attwood's off – have a bit of beefsteak?'

'What do you mean?' exclaimed I, adopting the familiar phraseology of my acquaintances: – 'Attwood off? – has he cut his stick?'[19]

'Not bad,' said the feeling and elegant Fips – 'not such a bad guess, my boy; but he has not exactly *cut his stick.*'

'What then?'

'*Why, his throat.*' The man's mouth was full of bleeding beef as he uttered this gentlemanly witticism.

I wish I could say that I was myself in the least affected by the news. I did not joke about it like my friend Fips; this was more for propriety's sake than for feeling's: but for my old school acquaintance, the friend of my early days, the merry associate of the last few months, I own, with shame, that I had not a tear or a pang. In some German tale there is an account of a creature most beautiful and bewitching, whom all men admire and follow; but this charming and fantastic spirit only leads them, one by one, into ruin, and then leaves them.[20] The novelist, who describes her beauty, says that his heroine is a fairy, and *has no heart*. I think the intimacy which is begotten over the wine-bottle, is a spirit of this nature; I never knew a good feeling come from it, or an honest friendship made by

19. Slang for 'gone on his way; left already'.
20. Thackeray ('Titmarsh') is, apparently, alluding to *The Devils' Elixirs* (1815), by E. T. A. Hoffmann.

it; it only entices men and ruins them; it is only a phantom of friendship and feeling, called up by the delirious blood, and the wicked spells of the wine.

But to drop this strain of moralizing (in which the writer is not too anxious to proceed, for he cuts in it a most pitiful figure), we passed sundry criticisms upon poor Attwood's character, expressed our horror at his death – which sentiment was fully proved by Mr Fips, who declared that the notion of it made him feel quite faint, and was obliged to drink a large glass of brandy; and, finally, we agreed that we would go and see the poor fellow's corpse, and witness, if necessary, his burial.

Flapper, who had joined us, was the first to propose this visit: he said he did not mind the fifteen francs which Jack owed him for billiards, but he was anxious to *get back his pistol.* Accordingly, we sallied forth, and speedily arrived at the hotel which Attwood inhabited still.

He had occupied, for a time, very fine apartments in this house: and it was only on arriving there that day that we found he had been gradually driven from his magnificent suite of rooms *au premier,*[21] to a little chamber in the fifth storey: – we mounted, and found him.

It was a little shabby room, with a few articles of rickety furniture, and a bed in an alcove; the light from

21. The first floor – usually the most expensive apartment.

the one window was falling full upon the bed and the body. Jack was dressed in a fine lawn shirt; he had kept it, poor fellow, *to die in*; for in all his drawers and cupboards there was not a single article of clothing; he had pawned everything by which he could raise a penny – desk, books, dressing-case, and clothes; and not a single halfpenny was found in his possession.[22]

He was lying one hand on his breast, the other falling towards the ground. There was an expression of perfect calm on the face, and no mark of blood to stain the side towards the light. On the other side, however, there was a great pool of black blood, and in it the pistol; it looked more like a toy than a weapon to take away the life of this vigorous young man. In his forehead, at the side, was a small black wound; Jack's life had passed through it; it was little bigger than a mole.

———

'*Regardez un peu,*' said the landlady, '*Messieurs, il m'a gâté trois matelas, et il me doit quarante quatre francs.*'

This was all his epitaph: he had spoiled three mattresses, and owed the landlady four-and-forty francs. In the whole world there was not a soul to love him or lament him. We, his friends, were looking at his body more as an object of curiosity, watching it with a kind of interest with which one follows the fifth act of a tragedy, and leaving it with the same feeling with

22. Thackeray's footnote: 'In order to account for these trivial details, the reader must be told that the story is, for the chief part, a fact.'

which one leaves the theatre when the play is over and the curtain is down.

Beside Jack's bed, on his little '*table de nuit*', lay the remains of his last meal, and an open letter, which we read. It was from one of his suspicious acquaintances of former days, and ran thus: –

'Où es tu, cher Jack? *why you not come and see me* – tu me dois de l'argent, entends tu? – un chapeau, une cachemire, *a box of the Play*. Viens demain soir, je t'attendrai *at eight o'clock*, Passage des Panoramas. *My Sir is at his country*.

'Adieu à demain. Fifine.'

'Samedi.'[23]

—

I shuddered as I walked through this very Passage des Panoramas, in the evening. The girl was there, pacing to and fro, and looking in the countenance of every passer-by, to recognize Attwood. 'Adieu à demain' – there was a dreadful meaning in the words, which the writer of them little knew. 'Adieu à demain!' – the morrow was come, and the soul of the poor suicide was now in the presence of God. I dare not think of his fate; for, except in the fact of his poverty and desperation, was he worse than any of us, his companions, who

23. Where are you my dear Jack . . . you owe me money, do you hear? – for a hat, a shawl . . . come tomorrow night. I'll be waiting at eight at Passage des Panoramas [the oldest covered mall in Paris]. My husband is out of town in the country. Goodbye till tomorrow, Fifine, Saturday.

had shared his debauches, and marched with him up to the very brink of the grave?

There is but one more circumstance to relate regarding poor Jack – his burial; it was of a piece with his death.

He was nailed into a paltry coffin and buried, at the expense of the arrondissement, in a nook of the burial-place beyond the Barrière de l'Etoile. They buried him at six o'clock, of a bitter winter's morning, and it was with difficulty that an English clergyman could be found to read a service over his grave. The three men who have figured in this history acted as Jack's mourners; and as the ceremony was to take place so early in the morning, these men sat up the night through, *and were almost drunk* as they followed his coffin to its resting-place.

MORAL

'When we turned out in our great-coats,' said one of them afterwards, 'reeking of cigars and brandy-and-water, d—e, sir, we quite frightened the old buck of a parson; he did not much like our company.' After the ceremony was concluded, these gentlemen were very happy to get home to a warm and comfortable breakfast, and finished the day royally at Frascati's.[24]

24. A fashionable restaurant on the Boulevard Montmartre.

– An Historical Study –

From *The Paris Sketch Book* (1844)

Ludovicus is Louis XIV: the Sun King. The triptych derives from Thomas Carlyle's satire on clothes, Sartor Resartus, *serialised earlier in* Fraser's Magazine. *Thackeray was more a cynic than a revolutionary – mockery, not the guillotine, is his killing weapon.*

REX — LUDOVICUS — LUDOVICUS REX

AN HISTORICAL STUDY

– On Going to See a Man Hanged –

Signed 'WMT' – from *Fraser's Magazine* (August 1840)

Thackeray attended the public execution here recorded on 4 July 1840, and wrote the essay while the experience was still hot in his mind. Until they were made illegal in 1868 'hang fairs' were popular 'entertainments of the people'. Tens of thousands would attend: whole families would make a picnic day of it. Dickens recorded that 'children would be held aloft at the critical moment to see how the gallows toy worked'. The dangling victim could take up to four minutes to stop 'dancing'. For the further delectation of the crowd, the body was left dangling at the end of the rope for an hour. The public execution Thackeray witnessed was that of François Benjamin Courvoisier, outside Newgate Prison.

Courvoisier, a Swiss valet who had cut his master Lord William Russell's throat, claimed, absurdly, to have been instigated to his savage crime by reading Harrison Ainsworth's 'Newgate' crime-novel, Jack Sheppard *(1839). The real motive was robbery. But the notion that fiction could be held responsible in this way intrigued Thackeray and partly motivated his attending this gruesome event.*

Thackeray, unlike Dickens, was an opponent of capital punishment: more so of hang fairs and what they did to spectators. His reasons are spelled out in this powerful essay.

X —,[1] who had voted with Mr Ewart[2] for the abolition of the punishment of death, was anxious to see the effect on the public mind of an execution, and asked me to accompany him to see Courvoisier killed. We had not the advantage of a sheriff's order, like the 'six hundred noblemen and gentlemen' who were admitted within the walls of the prison; but determined to mingle with the crowd at the foot of the scaffold, and take up our positions at a very early hour.

As I was to rise at three in the morning, I went to bed at ten, thinking that five hours' sleep would be amply sufficient to brace me against the fatigues of the coming day. But, as might have been expected, the event of the morrow was perpetually before my eyes through the night, and kept them wide open. I heard all the clocks in the neighbourhood chime the hours in succession; a dog from some court hard by kept up a pitiful howling; at one o'clock, a cock set up a feeble melancholy crowing; shortly after two the daylight came peeping grey through the window-shutters; and by the time that X— arrived, in fulfilment of his promise, I had been asleep about half-an-hour. He, more wise, had not gone to rest at all, but had remained up all night at the Club along with Dash and two or three

1. Richard Monckton Milnes, a friend of Thackeray's from their time together at Trinity College, Cambridge. At this period Milnes was a Tory MP.
2. William Ewart, a liberal campaigner in Parliament for the abolition of capital punishment – an unpopular cause – gave a speech on the subject on 23 June 1840, a few days before this public execution.

more. Dash is one of the most eminent wits in London, and had kept the company merry all night with appropriate jokes about the coming event. It is curious that a murder is a great inspirer of jokes. We all like to laugh and have our fling about it; there is a certain grim pleasure in the circumstance – a perpetual jingling antithesis between life and death, that is sure of its effect.

In mansion or garret, on down or straw, surrounded by weeping friends and solemn oily doctors, or tossing unheeded upon scanty hospital beds, there were many people in this great city to whom that Sunday night was to be the last of any that they should pass on earth here. In the course of half-a-dozen dark wakeful hours, one had leisure to think of these (and a little, too, of that certain supreme night, that shall come at one time or other, when he who writes shall be stretched upon the last bed, prostrate in the last struggle, taking the last look of dear faces that have cheered us here, and lingering – one moment more – ere we part for the tremendous journey); but, chiefly, I could not help thinking, as each clock sounded, what is *he* doing now – has *he* heard it in his little room in Newgate yonder – Eleven o'clock. He has been writing until now, can hold out no longer, and is very weary. 'Wake me at four,' says he, 'for I have still much to put down.' From eleven to twelve the gaoler hears how he is grinding his teeth in his sleep. At twelve he is up in his bed and asks, 'Is it the time?'

He has plenty more time yet for sleep; and he sleeps, and the bell goes on tolling. Seven hours more – five hours more. Many a carriage is clattering through the streets, bringing ladies away from evening parties; many bachelors are reeling home after a jolly night; Covent Garden is alive; and the light coming through the cell-window turns the gaoler's candle pale. Four hours more! 'Courvoisier,' says the gaoler, shaking him, 'it's four o'clock now, and I've woke you as you told me; but there's no call for you *to get up yet*.' The poor wretch leaves his bed, however, and makes his last toilet; and then falls to writing, to tell the world how he did the crime for which he has suffered. This time he will tell the truth and the whole truth. They bring him his breakfast 'from the coffee-shop opposite – tea, coffee, and thin bread and butter.' He will take nothing, however, but goes on writing. He has to write to his mother – the pious mother far away in his own country – who reared him and loved him; and even now has sent him her forgiveness and her blessing. He finishes his memorials and letters, and makes his will, disposing of his little miserable property of books and tracts that pious people have furnished him with. '*Ce 6 Juillet,* 1840. *François Benjamin Courvoisier vous donne çeçi, mon ami, pour souvenir.*'[3] He has a token for his dear friend the gaoler; another for his dear friend the under-sheriff. As the day of the

---

3. I give this to you my friend as a remembrance.

convict's death draws nigh, it is painful to see how he fastens upon everybody who approaches him, how pitifully he clings to them and loves them.

While these things are going on within the prison (with which we are made accurately acquainted by the copious chronicles of such events which are published subsequently), X—'s carriage has driven up to the door of my lodgings, and we have partaken of an elegant *dejeuner* that has been prepared for the occasion. A cup of coffee at half-past three in the morning is uncommonly pleasant; and X— enlivens us with the repetition of the jokes that Dash has just been making. Admirable, certainly – they must have had a merry night of it, that's clear; and we stoutly debate whether, when one has to get up so early in the morning, it is best to have an hour or two of sleep, or wait and go to bed afterwards at the end of the day's work. That fowl is extraordinarily tough – the wing, even, is as hard as a board; a slight disappointment, for there is nothing else for breakfast. 'Will any gentleman have some sherry and soda-water before he sets out? It clears the brains famously.' Thus primed, the party sets out. The coachman has dropped asleep on the box, and wakes up wildly as the hall-door opens. It is just four o'clock.

About this very time they are waking up poor – pshaw! who is for a cigar? X— does not smoke himself; but vows and protests, in the kindest way in the world, that he does not care in the least for the new drab-silk linings in his carriage. Z—, who smokes, mounts, however, the box. 'Drive to Snow Hill,' says the owner of the chariot. The policemen, who are the only people in the street, and are standing by, look knowing – they know what it means well enough.

How cool and clean the streets look, as the carriage startles the echoes that have been asleep in the corners all night. Somebody has been sweeping the pavements clean in the night-time surely; they would not soil a lady's white satin shoes, they are so dry and neat. There is not a cloud or a breath in the air, except Z—'s cigar, which whiffs off, and soars straight upwards in volumes of white pure smoke. The trees in the squares look bright and green – as bright as leaves in the country in June. We who keep late hours don't know the beauty of London air and verdure; in the early morning they are delightful – the most fresh and lively companions possible. But they cannot bear the crowd and the bustle of mid-day. You don't know them then – they are no longer the same things. We have come to Gray's Inn; there is actually dew upon the grass in the gardens; and the windows of the stout old red houses are all in a flame.

As we enter Holborn the town grows more animated; and there are already twice as many people in the streets as you see at mid-day in a German *Residenz* or an English provincial town. The ginshop keepers have many of them taken their shutters down, and many persons are issuing from them pipe in hand. Down they go along the broad bright street, their blue shadows marching *after* them; for they are all bound the same way, and are bent like us upon seeing the hanging.

It is twenty minutes past four as we pass St Sepulchre's: by this time many hundred people are in the street, and many more are coming up Snow Hill. Before us lies Newgate Prison; but something a great deal more awful to look at, which seizes the eye at once, and makes the heart beat, is . . .

There it stands black and ready, jutting out from a little door in the prison. As you see it, you feel a kind of dumb electric shock, which causes one to start a little, and give a sort of gasp for breath. The shock is over in a second; and presently you examine the object before you with a certain feeling of complacent curiosity. At least, such was the effect that the gallows produced upon the writer, who is trying to set down all his feelings as they occurred, and not to exaggerate them at all.

After the gallows-shock had subsided, we went down into the crowd, which was very numerous, but not dense as yet. It was evident that the day's business had not begun. People sauntered up, and formed groups, and talked; the new-comers asking those who seemed *habitués* of the place about former executions; and did the victim hang with his face towards the clock or towards Ludgate Hill? and had he the rope round his neck when he came on the scaffold, or was it put on by Jack Ketch[4] afterwards? and had Lord W— taken a window, and which was he? I may mention the noble Marquis's name, as he was not at the exhibition. A pseudo W— was pointed out in an opposite window, towards whom all the people in our neighbourhood looked eagerly, and with great respect too. The mob seemed to have no sort of ill-will against him, but sympathy and admiration. This noble lord's personal courage and strength have won the plebs over to him. Perhaps his exploits against policemen have occasioned some of this popularity; for the mob hate them, as children the schoolmaster.

Throughout the whole four hours, however, the mob was extraordinarily gentle and good-humoured. At first we had leisure to talk to the people about us; and I recommend X—'s brother senators of both sides of the House to see more of this same people and to appreciate them better. Honourable Members are bat-

4. Jack Ketch, famous as Charles II's executioner: his name served as a nickname for all in his grisly trade. Courvoisier was actually hanged by William Calcraft, notorious for his 'short drops', which would not break the condemned man's neck, but leave him to dangle and strangle. He gave the crowd good value.

tling and struggling in the House; shouting, yelling, crowing, hear-hearing, pooh-poohing, making speeches of three columns, and gaining 'great Conservative triumphs', or 'signal successes of the Reform cause', as the case may be. Three hundred and ten gentlemen of good fortune, and able for the most part to quote Horace, declare solemnly that unless Sir Robert[5] comes in, the nation is ruined. Three hundred and fifteen on the other side swear by their great gods that the safety of the empire depends upon Lord John;[6] and to this end they quote Horace too. I declare that I have never been in a great London crowd without thinking of what they call the two 'great' parties in England with wonder. For which of the two great leaders do these people care, I pray you? When Lord Stanley withdrew his Irish Bill[7] the other night, were they in transports of joy, like worthy persons who read the *Globe* and the *Chronicle*? or when he beat the Ministers, were they wild with delight, like honest gentlemen who read the *Post* and the *Times*? Ask yonder ragged fellow, who has evidently frequented debating-clubs, and speaks with good sense and shrewd good-nature. He cares no more for Lord John than he does for Sir Robert; and, with

5. Robert Peel, Conservative senior politician, sometime Prime Minister (1841–46).
6. Lord John Russell, senior Liberal politician, sometime Prime Minister, currently leader of the opposition.
7. Edward Smith-Stanley, 14th Earl of Derby. A senior Tory MP, Stanley withdrew his Irish Registration Bill (which would have rationalised Irish voting regulation) in late May 1840.

due respect be it said, would mind very little if both of them were ushered out by Mr Ketch, and took their places under yonder black beam. What are the two great parties to him, and those like him? Sheer wind, hollow humbug, absurd clap-traps; a silly mummery of dividing and debating, which does not in the least, however it may turn, affect his condition. It has been so ever since the happy days when Whigs and Tories began; and a pretty pastime no doubt it is for both. August parties, great balances of British freedom: are not the two sides quite as active, and eager, and loud, as at their very birth, and ready to fight for place as stoutly as ever they fought before? But lo! in the meantime, whilst you are jangling and brawling over the accounts, Populus, whose estate you have administered while he was an infant, and could not take care of himself – Populus , has been growing and growing, till he is every bit as wise as his guardians. Talk to our ragged friend. He is not so polished, perhaps, as a member of the 'Oxford and Cambridge Club'; he has not been to Eton; and never read Horace in his life; but he can think just as soundly as the best of you; he can speak quite as strongly in his own rough way; he has been reading all sorts of books of late years, and gathered together no little information. He is as good a man as the common run of us; and there are ten million more men in the country, as good as he – ten million, for whom we, in our infinite superiority, are acting as guardians, and to whom, in our bounty, we give –

exactly nothing. Put yourself in their position, worthy sir. You and a hundred others find yourselves in some lone place, where you set up a government. You take a chief, as is natural; he is the cheapest order-keeper in the world. You establish half-a-dozen worthies, whose families you say shall have the privilege to legislate for you forever; half-a-dozen more, who shall be appointed by a choice of thirty of the rest: and the other sixty, who shall have no choice, vote, place, or privilege at all. Honourable sir, suppose that you are one of the last sixty: how will you feel, you who have intelligence, passions, honest pride, as well as your neighbour; how will you feel towards your equals, in whose hands lie all the power and all the property of the community – Would you love and honour them, tamely acquiesce in their superiority, see their privileges, and go yourself disregarded without a pang? you are not a man if you would. I am not talking of right or wrong, or debating questions of government. But ask my friend there, with the ragged elbows and no shirt, what he thinks – You have your party, Conservative or Whig, as it may be. You believe that an aristocracy is an institution necessary, beautiful, and virtuous. You are a gentleman, in other words, and stick by your party.

And our friend with the elbows (the crowd is thickening hugely all this time) sticks by *his*. Talk to him of Whig or Tory, he grins at them: of virtual representation, pish! He is a *democrat*, and will stand by his friends, as you by yours; and they are twenty millions, his friends, of whom a vast minority now, a majority a few years hence, will be as good as you. In the meantime we shall continue electing, and debating, and dividing, and having every day new triumphs for the glorious cause of Conservatism, or the glorious cause of Reform, until −

—

What is the meaning of this unconscionable republican tirade − *à propos* of a hanging? Such feelings, I think, must come across any man in a vast multitude like this. What good sense and intelligence have most of the people by whom you are surrounded; how much sound humour does one hear bandied about from one to another! A great number of coarse phrases are used, that would make ladies in drawing-rooms blush; but the morals of the men are good and hearty. A ragamuffin in the crowd (a powdery baker in a white sheep's-wool cap) uses some indecent expression to a woman near: there is an instant cry of shame, which silences the man, and a dozen people are ready to give the woman protection. The crowd has grown very dense by this time, it is about six o'clock, and there is great heaving, and pushing, and swaying to and fro; but round the women the men have formed a circle, and keep them as much as possible out of the rush and trample. In one of the houses, near us, a gallery has been formed on the roof. Seats were here let, and a number of persons of various degrees were occupying

them. Several tipsy dissolute-looking young men, of
the Dick Swiveller cast,[8] were in this gallery. One was
lolling over the sunshiny tiles, with a fierce sodden
face, out of which came a pipe, and which was shaded
by long matted hair, and a hat cocked very much on
one side. This gentleman was one of a party which had
evidently not been to bed on Sunday night, but had
passed it in some of those delectable night-houses in
the neighbourhood of Covent Garden. The debauch
was not over yet, and the women of the party were gig-
gling, drinking, and romping, as is the wont of these
delicate creatures; sprawling here and there, and falling upon the knees of one or other of the males. Their
scarves were off their shoulders, and you saw the sun
shining down upon the bare white flesh, and the shoul-
der-points glittering like burning-glasses. The people
about us were very indignant at some of the proceedings of this debauched crew, and at last raised up such
a yell as frightened them into shame, and they were
more orderly for the remainder of the day. The windows of the shops opposite began to fill apace, and our
before-mentioned friend with ragged elbows pointed
out a celebrated fashionable character who occupied
one of them; and, to our surprise, knew as much about
him as the *Court Journal* or the *Morning Post*. Presently he entertained us with a long and pretty accurate
account of the history of Lady—, and indulged in a

8. An amiable character in Dickens's *Old Curiosity Shop*, being serialised at the time of Thackeray writing this.

judicious criticism upon her last work. I have met with many a country gentleman who had not read half as many books as this honest fellow, this shrewd *proletaire* in a black shirt.[9] The people about him took up and carried on the conversation very knowingly, and were very little behind him in point of information. It was just as good a company as one meets on common occasions. I was in a genteel crowd in one of the galleries at the Queen's coronation;[10] indeed, in point of intelligence, the democrats were quite equal to the aristocrats. How many more such groups were there in this immense multitude of nearly forty thousand, as some say – How many more such throughout the country? I never yet, as I said before, have been in an English mob without the same feeling for the persons who composed it, and without wonder at the vigorous orderly good sense and intelligence of the people.

The character of the crowd was as yet, however, quite festive. Jokes bandying about here and there, and jolly laughs breaking out. Some men were endeavouring to climb up a leaden pipe on one of the houses. The landlord came out, and endeavoured with might and main to pull them down. Many thousand eyes turned upon this contest immediately. All sorts of voices issued from the crowd, and uttered choice expressions of slang. When one of the men was pulled down by the leg, the waves of this black mob-ocean laughed

9. A black shirt and black flag was the uniform of the political radical.
10. Queen Victoria's coronation took place on 28 June 1838.

innumerably; when one fellow slipped away, scrambled up the pipe, and made good his lodgment on the shelf, we were all made happy, and encouraged him by loud shouts of admiration. What is there so particularly delightful in the spectacle of a man clambering up a gaspipe? Why were we kept for a quarter of an hour in deep interest gazing upon this remarkable scene? Indeed it is hard to say: a man does not know what a fool he is until he tries; or, at least, what mean follies will amuse him. The other day I went to Astley's[11] and saw a clown come in with a fool's-cap and pinafore, and six small boys who represented his schoolfellows. To them enters schoolmaster; horses clown, and flogs him hugely on the back part of his pinafore. I never read anything in Swift, Boz, Rabelais, Fielding, Paul de Kock,[12] which delighted me so much as this sight, and caused me to laugh so profoundly. And why? What is there so ridiculous in the sight of one miserably rouged man beating another on the breech? Tell us where the fun lies in this and the before-mentioned episode of the gas-pipe? Vast, indeed, are the capacities and ingenuities of the human soul that can find, in incidents so wonderfully

11. Astley's Amphitheatre, in London, famous for its circus entertainments and horse-acts. Dickens wrote about it in *Sketches by Boz* (1836) and devotes a chapter to it in *The Old Curiosity Shop*.
12. The name in this list which may not be recognised by the general reader is Paul de Kock, whom Thackeray often references. A voluminously productive French novelist, de Kock's works translated well and were regarded as just this side of licentious for the English Victorian reader.

small, means of contemplation and amusement.

Really the time passed away with extraordinary quickness. A thousand things of the sort related here came to amuse us. First the workmen knocking and hammering at the scaffold, mysterious clattering of blows was heard within it, and a ladder painted black was carried round, and into the interior of the edifice by a small side door. We all looked at this little ladder and at each other – things began to be very interesting. Soon came a squad of policemen; stalwart rosy-looking men, saying much for City feeding; well-dressed, well-limbed, and of admirable good-humour. They paced about the open space between the prison and the barriers which kept in the crowd from the scaffold. The front line, as far as I could see, was chiefly occupied by blackguards and boys – professional persons, no doubt, who saluted the policemen on their appearance with a volley of jokes and ribaldry. As far as I could judge from faces, there were more blackguards of sixteen and seventeen than of any maturer age; stunted, sallow, ill-grown lads, in ragged fustian, scowling about. There were a considerable number of girls, too, of the same age: one that Cruikshank and Boz might have taken as a study for Nancy.[13] The girl was a young

13. Nancy is the thief Bill Sikes's street-walker moll in *Oliver Twist*. Dickens ('Boz', illustrared by George Cruikshank), who was among the 40,000-strong crowd watching Courvoisier's execution, took great offence at this reference to his novel – more so as it was, like Harrison Ainsworth's *Jack Sheppard*, the kind of 'Newgate Novel' Courvoisier claimed had driven him to his crime.

thief's mistress evidently; if attacked, ready to reply without a particle of modesty; could give as good ribaldry as she got; made no secret (and there were several inquiries) as to her profession and means of livelihood. But with all this, there was something good about the girl; a sort of devil-may-care candour and simplicity that one could not fail to see. Her answers to some of the coarse questions put to her, were very ready and good-humoured. She had a friend with her of the same age and class, of whom she seemed to be very fond, and who looked up to her for protection. Both of these women had beautiful eyes. Devil-may-care's were extraordinarily bright and blue, an admirably fair complexion, and a large red mouth full of white teeth. *Au reste*, ugly, stunted, thick-limbed, and by no means a beauty. Her friend could not be more than fifteen. They were not in rags, but had greasy cotton shawls, and old faded rag-shop bonnets. I was curious to look at them, having, in late fashionable novels, read many accounts of such personages. Bah! what figments these novelists tell us! Boz, who knows life well, knows that his Miss Nancy is the most unreal fantastical personage possible; no more like a thief's mistress than one of Gesner's shepherdesses[14] resembles a real country wench. He dare not tell the truth concerning such young ladies. They have, no doubt, virtues like other

14. Solomon Gesner (1730–88), Swiss painter and poet, much admired in his day for his poems and paintings celebrating imaginary pastoral life.

human creatures; nay, their position engenders virtues that are not called into exercise among other women. But on these an honest painter of human nature has no right to dwell; not being able to paint the whole portrait, he has no right to present one or two favourable points as characterising the whole; and therefore, in fact, had better leave the picture alone altogether. The new French literature is essentially false and worthless from this very error – the writers giving us favourable pictures of monsters, and (to say nothing of decency or morality) pictures quite untrue to nature.

But yonder, glittering through the crowd in Newgate Streets – see, the Sheriff's carriages are slowly making their way. We have been here three hours! Is it possible that they can have passed so soon? Close to the barriers where we are, the mob has become so dense that it is with difficulty a man can keep his feet. Each man, however, is very careful in protecting the women, and all are full of jokes and good-humour. The windows of the shops opposite are now pretty nearly filled by the persons who hired them. Many young dandies are there with moustaches and cigars; some quiet fat family-parties, of simple honest tradesmen and their wives, as we fancy, who are looking on with the greatest imaginable calmness, and sipping their tea. Yonder is the sham Lord W—, who is flinging various articles among the crowd; one of his companions, a tall, burly man, with large moustaches, has provided himself with a squirt, and is aspersing the mob with brandy-and-water. Honest gentleman! high-bred aristocrat! genuine lover of humour and wit! I would walk some miles to see thee on the treadmill, thee and thy Mohawk crew![15]

We tried to get up a hiss against these ruffians, but only had a trifling success; the crowd did not seem to think their offence very heinous; and our friend, the philosopher in the ragged elbows, who had remained near us all the time, was not inspired with any such savage disgust at the proceedings of certain notorious young gentlemen, as I must confess fills my own particular bosom. He only said, 'So-and-so is a lord, and they'll let him off,' and then discoursed about Lord Ferrers[16] being hanged. The philosopher knew the history pretty well, and so did most of the little knot of persons about him, and it must be a gratifying thing for young gentlemen to find that their actions are made the subject of this kind of conversation.

Scarcely a word had been said about Courvoisier all this time. We were all, as far as I could judge, in just such a frame of mind as men are in when they are squeezing at the pit-door of a play, or pushing for a review or a Lord Mayor's show. We asked most of the men who were near us, whether they had seen many executions? most of them had, the philosopher

15. Mohawk: an eighteenth-century term for high-born street rowdies.
16. Earl Ferrers (1720–60), the last aristocrat to be hanged in Britain. The dissolute, possibly mad, Ferrers murdered his steward over money and was condemned to hang by his fellow peers at Westminster. As was his birthright, he was hanged by a silk rope.

especially; whether the sight of them did any good? 'For the matter of that, no; people did not care about them at all; nobody ever thought of it after a bit.' A countryman, who had left his drove in Smithfield, said the same thing; he had seen a man hanged at York, and spoke of the ceremony with perfect good sense, and in a quiet sagacious way.

J. S—, the famous wit, now dead, had, I recollect, a good story upon the subject of executing, and of the terror which the punishment inspires. After Thistlewood[17] and his companions were hanged, their heads were taken off, according to the sentence, and the executioner, as he severed each, held it up to the crowd, in the proper orthodox way, saying, 'Here is the head of a traitor!' At the sight of the first ghastly head the people were struck with terror, and a general expression of disgust and fear broke from them. The second head was looked at also with much interest, but the excitement regarding the third head diminished. When the executioner had come to the last of the heads, he lifted it up, but, by some clumsiness, allowed it to drop. At this the crowd yelled out, *'Ah, Butter-fingers!'* the excitement had passed entirely away. The punishment

17. Arthur Thistlewood was the head of the so-called Cato Street conspiracy, a band of radicals who aimed to assassinate the then Prime Minister Lord Liverpool in 1820. The gang was infiltrated by the authorities who took early and wholly effective action. During his arrest Thistlewood killed a police officer. The ancient punishment of hanging, drawing and quartering was commuted, but five of the gang were hanged at Newgate and decapitated after death.

had grown to be a joke – Butter-fingers was the word – a pretty commentary, indeed, upon the august nature of public executions, and the awful majesty of the law.

It was past seven now; the quarters rang and passed away; the crowd began to grow very eager and more quiet, and we turned back every now and then and looked at St Sepulchre's clock. Half-an-hour, twenty-five minutes. What is he doing now? He has his irons off by this time. A quarter: he's in the press-room[18] now, no doubt. Now at last we had come to think about the man we were going to see hanged. How slowly the clock crept over the last quarter! Those who were able to turn round and see (for the crowd was now extraordinarily dense) chronicled the time, eight minutes, five minutes; at last – ding, dong, dong, dong! – the bell is tolling the chimes of eight.

—

Between the writing of this line and the last, the pen has been put down, as the reader may suppose, and the person who is addressing him has gone through a pause of no very pleasant thoughts and recollections. The whole of the sickening, ghastly, wicked scene passes before the eyes again; and, indeed, it is an awful one to see, and very hard and painful to describe.

As the clock began to strike, an immense sway

18. The press room, so called, was where prisoners who did not confess to their crime were, in past times, 'pressed', or crushed, with heavy stones to make them do so.

and movement swept over the whole of that vast dense crowd. They were all uncovered directly, and a great murmur arose, more awful, bizarre, and indescribable than any sound I had ever before heard. Women and children began to shriek horribly. I don't know whether it was the bell I heard; but a dreadful quick feverish kind of jangling noise mingled with the noise of the people, and lasted for about two minutes. The scaffold stood before us, tenantless and black; the black chain was hanging down ready from the beam. Nobody came. 'He has been respited,' some one said; another said, 'He has killed himself in prison.'[19]

Just then, from under the black prison-door, a pale quiet head peered out. It was shockingly bright and distinct; it rose up directly, and a man in black appeared on the scaffold, and was silently followed by about four more dark figures. The first was a tall grave man: we all knew who the second man was. *That's he – that's he!*' you heard the people say, as the devoted man came up.

I have seen a cast of the head since, but, indeed, should never have known it.[20] Courvoisier bore his punishment like a man, and walked very firmly. He was dressed in a new black suit, as it seemed: his shirt was

19. Courvoisier did attempt to kill himself on the night before execution with a piece of sharpened wood. He was discovered bleeding, bandaged and made to spend his last night on earth sleeping naked.
20. A cast was taken of Courvoisier's head and was written about by the phrenologist John Elliotson, a friend of both Dickens and Thackeray.

open. His arms were tied in front of him. He opened
his hands in a helpless kind of way, and clasped them
once or twice together. He turned his head here and
there, and looked about him for an instant with a wild
imploring look. His mouth was contracted into a sort
of pitiful smile. He went and placed himself at once
under the beam, with his face towards St Sepulchre's.
The tall grave man in black twisted him round swiftly
in the other direction, and, drawing from his pocket
a night-cap, pulled it tight over the patient's head and
face. I am not ashamed to say that I could look no
more, but shut my eyes as the last dreadful act was going on which sent this wretched guilty soul into the
presence of God.

If a public execution is beneficial – and beneficial it is, no doubt, or else the wise laws would not
encourage forty thousand people to witness it – the
next useful thing must be a full description of such
a ceremony, and all its *entourages*, and to this end the
above pages are offered to the reader. How does an
individual man feel under it? In what way does he
observe it, – how does he view all the phenomena
connected with it, – what induces him, in the first instance, to go and see it, – and how is he moved by it
afterwards? The writer has discarded the magazine
'We' altogether, and spoken face to face with the reader, recording every one of the impressions felt by him
as honestly as he could.

I must confess, then (for 'I' is the shortest word,

and the best in this case), that the sight has left on my mind an extraordinary feeling of terror and shame. It seems to me that I have been abetting an act of frightful wickedness and violence, performed by a set of men against one of their fellows; and I pray God that it may soon be out of the power of any man in England to witness such a hideous and degrading sight. Forty thousand persons (say the Sheriffs), of all ranks and degrees, – mechanics, gentlemen, pickpockets, members of both Houses of Parliament, street-walkers, newspaper-writers, gather together before Newgate at a very early hour; the most part of them give up their natural quiet night's rest, in order to partake of this hideous debauchery, which is more exciting than sleep, or than wine, or the last new ballet, or any other amusement they can have. Pickpocket and Peer each is tickled by the sight alike, and has that hidden lust after blood which influences our race. Government, a Christian Government, gives us a feast every now and then: it agrees – that is to say, a majority in the two Houses agrees – that for certain crimes it is necessary that a man should be hanged by the neck. Government commits the criminal's soul to the mercy of God, stating that here on earth he is to look for no mercy; keeps him for a fortnight to prepare, provides him with a clergymen to settle his religious matters (if there be time enough, but Government can't wait); and on a Monday morning, the bell tolling, the clergyman reading out the word of God, 'I am the resurrection and the life,' 'The Lord giveth and the Lord taketh away,' – on a Monday morning, at eight o'clock, this man is placed under a beam, with a rope connecting it and him; a plank disappears from under him, and those who have paid for good places may see the hands of the Government agent, Jack Ketch, coming up from his black hole, and seizing the prisoner's legs, and pulling them, until he is quite dead – strangled.[21]

Many persons, and well-informed newspapers, say that it is mawkish sentiment to talk in this way, morbid humanity, cheap philanthropy, that any man can get up and preach about. There is the *Observer*, for instance, a paper conspicuous for the tremendous sarcasm which distinguishes its articles, and which falls cruelly foul of the *Morning Herald*. 'Courvoisier is dead,' says the *Observer*: 'he died as he had lived – a villain; a lie was in his mouth. Peace be to his ashes. We war not with the dead.' What a magnanimous *Observer*! From this, *Observer* turns to the *Herald*, and says, 'Fiat justitia, ruat cælum.'[22] So much for the *Herald*.

We quote from memory, and the quotation from the *Observer* possibly is, – De mortuis nil nisi bonum; or, Omne ignotum pro magnifico; or, Sero nunquam est ad bonos mores via; or, Ingenuas didicisse fideliter artes emollit mores nec sinit esse feros: all of which

---

21. Calcraft was typically inept, giving Courvoisier a short drop which strangled but did not break his neck. Tugging on his legs, out of public sight, mercifully speeded strangulation.
22. 'Let justice be done though the heavens fall.'

pithy Roman apophthegms would apply just as well.[23]

'Peace be to his ashes. He died, a villain.' This is both benevolence and reason. Did he die a villain? The *Observer* does not want to destroy him body and soul, evidently, from that pious wish that his ashes should be at peace. Is the next Monday but one after the sentence the time necessary for a villain to repent in? May a man not require more leisure – a week more – six months more – before he has been able to make his repentance sure before Him who died for us all? – for all, be it remembered, – not alone for the judge and jury, or for the sheriffs, or for the executioner who is pulling down the legs of the prisoner, – but for him too, murderer and criminal as he is, whom we are killing for his crime. Do we want to kill him body and soul? Heaven forbid! My Lord in the black cap specially prays that Heaven may have mercy on him; but he must be ready by Monday morning.

Look at the documents which came from the prison of this unhappy Courvoisier during the few days which passed between his trial and execution. Were ever letters more painful to read? At first, his statements are false, contradictory, lying. He has not repented then. His last declaration seems to be honest, as far as the relation of the crime goes. But read the rest of his statement, the account of his personal

23. The Latin in this paragraph means, loosely, 'speak no ill of the dead'; 'every unknown thing becomes wonderful'; 'It is never too late to do the right thing'; 'Good influence softens savagery'.

history, and the crimes which he committed in his young days, – then 'how the evil thought came to him to put his hand to the work,' – it is evidently the writing of a mad, distracted man. The horrid gallows is perpetually before him; he is wild with dread and remorse. Clergymen are with him ceaselessly; religious tracts are forced into his hands; night and day they ply him with the heinousness of his crime, and exhortations to repentance. Read through that last paper of his; by Heaven, it is pitiful to read it. See the Scripture phrases brought in now and anon; the peculiar terms of tract-phraseology (I do not wish to speak of these often meritorious publications with disrespect); one knows too well how such language is learned, – imitated from the priest at the bedside, eagerly seized and appropriated, and confounded by the poor prisoner.

But murder is such a monstrous crime (this is the great argument), – when a man has killed another it is natural that he should be killed. Away with your foolish sentimentalists who say no – it is *natural*. That is the word, and a fine philosophical opinion it is – philosophical and Christian. Kill a man and you must be killed in turn: that is the unavoidable *sequitur*. You may talk to a man for a year upon the subject, and he will always reply to you, 'It is natural, and therefore it must be done. Blood demands blood.'

Does it? The system of compensations might be carried on *ad infinitum*, – an eye for an eye, a tooth for a tooth, as by the old Mosaic law. But (putting the fact out of the question, that we have had this statute repealed by the Highest Authority[24]), why, because you lose your eye, is that of your opponent to be extracted likewise? Where is the reason for the practice? And yet it is just as natural as the death dictum, founded precisely upon the same show of sense. Knowing, however, that revenge is not only evil, but useless, we have given it up on all minor points. Only to the last we stick firm, contrary though it be to reason and to Christian law.

There is some talk, too, of the terror which the sight of this spectacle inspires, and of this we have endeavoured to give as good a notion as we can in the above pages. I fully confess that I came away down Snow Hill that morning with a disgust for murder, but it was for *the murder I saw done.* As we made our way through the immense crowd, we came upon two little girls of eleven and twelve years: one of them was crying bitterly, and begged, for Heaven's sake, that some one would lead her from that horrid place. This was done, and the children were carried into a place of safety. We asked the elder girl – and a very pretty one – what brought her into such a neighbourhood? The child grinned knowingly, and said, 'We've koom to see the mon hanged!' Tender law, that brings out babes upon such errands, and provides them with such gratifying moral spectacles!

24. Jesus Christ.

46

This is the 20th of July, and I may be permitted for my part to declare that, for the last fourteen days, so salutary has the impression of the butchery been upon me, I have had the man's face continually before my eyes; that I can see Mr Ketch at this moment, with an easy air, taking the rope from his pocket; that I feel myself ashamed and degraded at the brutal curiosity which took me to that brutal sight; and that I pray to Almighty God to cause this disgraceful sin to pass from among us, and to cleanse our land of blood.

– Little Billee –

(1845)

This impromptu ballad was composed in the early 1840s. Thackeray was making his name (behind his barrage of pseudonymy) as a wit and a journalist. He was now a lead writer (and cartoonist) in the new magazine, Punch. *At evening meetings of the magazine confrères, over drinks and tobacco, Thackeray would entertain the company with ballads such as this one.*

'Little Billee' belongs to the genre known as 'ruthless rhymes'. The background is given by Gordon Ray. Thackeray was travelling the Mediterranean in late 1844, writing travelogue pieces for Punch *under the pseudonym 'Our Fat Correspondent' (he was dining richly at this time of his life). At a dull dinner in Naples, as a friend recalled: 'Thackeray was voted into the chair for a round of "song and sentiment". He declined to sing, but he did offer a recitation. Thus was engendered Thackeray's most celebrated improvisation "The three sailors", which he delivered in a fittingly lugubrious tone of voice.'* [1]

In 'Il était un petit navire' (There was once a little sailor-boy), the popular French ballad Thackeray was closely imitating, the boy hero is saved by the Virgin Mary. Thackeray alters that, wittily, and bloodily.

1. Gordon Ray, *The Uses of Adversity.*

— *Little Billee* —

Air – '*il y avait un petit navire*'

T here were three sailors of Bristol City
    Who took a boat and went to sea,
But first with beef and captain's biscuits
    And pickled pork they loaded she.

There was gorging Jack, and guzzling Jimmy,
    And the youngster he was little Billee;
Now when they 'd got as far as the Equator,
    They'd nothing left but one split pea.

Says gorging Jack to guzzling Jimmy,
    'I am extremely hungaree.'
To gorging Jack says guzzling Jimmy,
    'We've nothing left, us must eat we.'[2]

Says gorging Jack to guzzling Jimmy,
    'With one another we shouldn't agree!
There 's little Bill, he 's young and tender,
    We're old and tough, so let's eat he.'

'O Billy! we're going to kill and eat you,
    So undo the button of your chemie.'
When Bill received this information,
    He used his pocket-handkerchie.

2. The so-called 'custom of the sea' was much discussed in the nineteenth century before being repealed. Essentially it sanctioned drawing of lots to warrant consensual cannibalism for survival in extreme distress or shipwreck.

'First let me say my catechism
   Which my poor mother taught to me.'
'Make haste! make haste!' says guzzling Jimmy,
   While Jack pulled out his snickersnee.

Billy went up to the main-top-gallant mast,
   And down he fell on his bended knee,
He scarce had come to the Twelfth Commandment
   When up he jumps – 'There's land I see!

'Jerusalem and Madagascar
   And North and South Amerikee,
There's the British flag a-riding at anchor,
   With Admiral Napier, K.C.B.'[3]

So when they got aboard of the Admiral's,
   He hanged fat Jack and flogged Jimmee,
But as for little Bill he made him
   The Captain of a Seventy-three.[4]

3. Admiral Sir Charles Napier, a long-serving nautical hero. He introduced a number of humane reforms into Navy law and was, at the
time Thackeray is writing, the most popular seaman in Britain.
4. i.e., a 73-gun vessel.

– Waterloo –

From *Little Travels and Roundabout Sketches* (1845)

This is the third and last chapter in Little Travels and
Roundabout Sketches, *first serialised in* Fraser's Magazine, *May 1843 to January 1845.*

   *This chapter is a commemoration of the great 1815
battle. But Thackeray is wilfully not flag-waving. Was
there not, he asks, something hollow in the national
jubilation about two great nations battling to see who
could lose most blood and end up victor?*

   *Thackeray here adapts his favourite alter-ego,
Michael Angelo Titmarsh, into the person of a gentleman tourist. The essay is addressed to Titmarsh's wife,
Juliana, recording what the men talk about after dinner
when the ladies have retired to the drawing room.*

I t is, my dear, the happy privilege of your sex in
  England to quit the dinner-table after the wine-
bottles have once or twice gone round it, and you are
thereby saved (though, to be sure, I can't tell what the
ladies do up stairs) – you are saved two or three hours'
excessive dulness, which the men are obliged to go
through.

   I ask any gentleman who reads this – the letters
to my Juliana being written with an eye to publication

– to remember especially how many times, how many hundred times, how many thousand times, in his hearing, the battle of Waterloo has been discussed after dinner, and to call to mind how cruelly he has been bored by the discussion. 'Ah, it was lucky for us that the Prussians came up!'[1] says one little gentleman, looking particularly wise and ominous. 'Hang the Prussians!' (or, perhaps, something stronger 'the Prussians!') says a stout old major on half-pay. 'We beat the French without them, sir, as beaten them we always have! We were thundering down the hill of Belle Alliance, sir, at the backs of them, and the French were crying *"Sauve qui peut"* long before the Prussians ever touched them!' And so the battle opens, and for many mortal hours, amid rounds of claret, rages over and over again.

I thought to myself considering the above things, what a fine thing it will be in after-days to say that I have been to Brussels and never seen the field of Waterloo; indeed, that I am such a philosopher as not to care a fig about the battle – nay, to regret, rather, that when Napoleon came back, the British Government had not spared their men and left him alone.

But this pitch of philosophy was unattainable. This morning, after having seen the Park, the fashionable boulevard, the pictures, the cafes – having sipped, I say, the sweets of every flower that grows in

1. The Prussian army, under Blücher, was late arriving at the battlefield but once there proved decisive – or so say the Germans.

this paradise of Brussels, quite weary of the place, we mounted on a Namur *diligence*,[2] and jingled off at four miles an hour for Waterloo.

The road is very neat and agreeable: the Forest of Soignies here and there interposes pleasantly, to give your vehicle a shade; the country, as usual, is vastly fertile and well cultivated. A farmer and the conducteur were my companions in the imperial, and could I have understood their conversation, my dear, you should have had certainly a report of it. The jargon which they talked was, indeed, most queer and puzzling – French, I believe, strangely hashed up and pronounced, for here and there one could catch a few words of it. Now and anon, however, they condescended to speak in the purest French they could muster; and, indeed, nothing is more curious than to hear the French of the country. You can't understand why all the people insist upon speaking it so badly. I asked the conductor if he had been at the battle; he burst out laughing like a philosopher, as he was, and said '*Pas si bête.*'[3] I asked the farmer whether his contributions were lighter now than in King William's time, and lighter than those in the time of the Emperor?[4] He vowed that in wartime he had not more to pay than in time of peace

2. The Namur *diligence* (a four-horse omnibus, nicknamed 'Dilly') ran a regular afternoon service from Namur to the battlefield for the tourist trade.
3. 'Not so stupid.'
4. For King William see following fooootnote 6; the Emperor Napoleon, commander at Waterloo.

(and this strange fact is vouched for by every person of every nation), and being asked wherefore the King of Holland had been ousted from his throne, replied at once, '*Parce que c'était un voleur:*'[5] for which accusation I believe there is some show of reason, his Majesty having laid hands on much Belgian property before the lamented outbreak which cost him his crown.[6] A vast deal of laughing and roaring passed between these two worldly people and the postilion, whom they called 'baron', and I thought no doubt that this talk was one of the many jokes that my companions were in the habit of making. But not so: the postilion was an actual baron, the bearer of an ancient name, the descendant of gallant gentlemen. Good heavens! what would Mrs Trollope say to see his lordship here?[7] His father the old baron had dissipated the family fortune, and here was this young nobleman, at about five-and-forty, compelled to bestride a clattering Flemish stallion, and bump over dusty pavements at the rate of five miles an hour. But see the beauty of high blood: with what a calm grace the man of family accommodates himself to fortune. Far from being cast down, his lordship met his fate like a man: he swore and laughed the

5. 'Because he was a thief.'
6. King William I of the Netherlands abdicated from a long reign in 1840 in the face of popular resentment at the 'loss' of an insurgent Belgium in 1839.
7. Anthony's Trollope's mother (Frances Milton Trollope). 'Mrs Trollope' supported the family by writing bestselling fiction and travel books. Thackeray refers here to her comic novel, *The Robertses on their Travels*. Belgium figures in it.

whole of the journey, and as we changed horses, condescended to partake of half a pint of Louvain beer, to which the farmer treated him – indeed the worthy rustic treated me to a glass too.

Much delight and instruction have I had in the course of the journey from my guide, philosopher, and friend, the author of 'Murray's Handbook'.[8] He has gathered together, indeed, a store of information, and must, to make his single volume, have gutted many hundreds of guide-books. How the Continental ciceroni[9] must hate him, whoever he is! Every English party I saw had this infallible red book in their hands, and gained a vast deal of historical and general information from it. Thus I heard, in confidence, many remarkable anecdotes of Charles V, the Duke of Alva, Count Egmont, all of which I had before perceived, with much satisfaction, not only in the *Handbook*, but even in other works.[10]

The Laureate is among the English poets evidently

8. John Murray's distinctively red-bound travel guides enjoyed biblical authority. Thackeray makes mocking reference over the next few hundred words to the 1845 *Handbook for Travellers on the Continent: Being a Guide through Holland, Belgium, and Northern Germany*.
9. Ciceroni – sightseers' personal guide.
10. Murray is informative about Charles V (1500–58), Holy Roman Emperor, one-time ruler of the Low Countries which he lost to Protestant uprising in 1556; the third Duke of Alba (i.e. Alva), was sent with an army by the Spanish monarch to suppress Protestant 'heresy' in 1567, which he did bloodily; among those he killed was Count Egmont – an act of unjustified brutality which provoked more uprising than it suppressed.

the great favourite of our guide: the choice does honour to his head and heart. A man must have a very strong bent for poetry, indeed, who carries Southey's[11] works in his portmanteau, and quotes them in proper time and occasion. Of course at Waterloo a spirit like our guide's cannot fail to be deeply moved, and to turn to his favourite poet for sympathy. Hark how the laureate bard sings about the tombstones at Waterloo: –

> That temple to our hearts was hallow'd now,
> For many a wounded Briton there was laid,
> With such for help as time might then allow,
> From the fresh carnage of the field conveyed.
> And they whom human succour could not save,
> Here, in its precincts, found a hasty grave.
> And here, on marble tablets, set on high,
> In English lines by foreign workmen traced,
> The names familiar to an English eye,
> Their brethren here the fit memorial placed;
> Whose unadorn'd inscriptions briefly tell
> *Their gallant comrades*' rank, and where they fell.
> The stateliest monument of human pride,
> Enriched with all magnificence of art,
> To honour chieftains who in victory died,
> Would wake no stronger feeling in the heart
> Than these plain tablets by the soldier's hand
> Raised to his comrades in a foreign land.

11. Robert Southey was Poet Laureate from 1813 to 1843. His patriotic verse 'The Poet's Pilgrimage to Waterloo', which Thackeray holds up for scorn here, is quoted at length in Murray.

There are lines for you! wonderful for justice, rich in thought and novel ideas. The passage concerning their gallant comrades' rank should be specially re-marked. There indeed they lie, sure enough: the Honorable Colonel This of the Guards, Captain That of the Hussars, Major So-and-So of the Dragoons, brave men and good, who did their duty by their country on that day, and died in the performance of it.

Amen. But I confess fairly, that in looking at these tablets, I felt very much disappointed at not seeing the names of the *men* as well as the officers. Are they to be counted for nought? A few more inches of marble to each monument would have given space for all the names of the men; and the men of that day were the winners of the battle. We have a right to be as grateful individually to any given private as to any given officer; their duties were very much the same. Why should the country reserve its gratitude for the genteel occupiers of the army-list, and forget the gallant fellows whose humble names were written in the regimental books? In reading of the Wellington wars, and the conduct of the men engaged in them, I don't know whether to respect them or to wonder at them most. They have death, wounds, and poverty in contemplation; in possession, poverty, hard labour, hard fare, and small thanks. If they do wrong, they are handed over to the inevitable provost-marshal;[12] if they are heroes, heroes

12. For flogging.

they may be, but they remain privates still, handling the old brown-bess,[13] starving on the old twopence a day. They grow grey in battle and victory, and after thirty years of bloody service, a young gentleman of fifteen, fresh from a preparatory school, who can scarcely read, and came but yesterday with a pinafore in to papa's dessert – such a young gentleman, I say, arrives in a spick-and-span red coat, and calmly takes the command over our veteran, who obeys him as if God and nature had ordained that so throughout time it should be.

That privates should obey, and that they should be smartly punished if they disobey, this one can understand very well. But to say obey for ever and ever – to say that Private John Styles is, by some physical disproportion, hopelessly inferior to Cornet Snooks – to say that Snooks shall have honors, epaulets, and a marble tablet if he dies, and that Styles shall fight his fight, and have his twopence a day, and when shot down shall be shovelled into a hole with other Styleses, and so forgotten; and to think that we had in the course of the last war some 400,000 of these Styleses, and some 10,000, say, of the Snooks sort – Styles being by nature exactly as honest, clever, and brave as Snooks – and to think that the 400,000 should bear this, is the wonder!

Suppose Snooks makes a speech. 'Look at these

13. Standard-issue musket to the British infantry from the 1720s to the 1830s.

Frenchmen, British soldiers,' says he, 'and remember who they are. Two-and-twenty years since they hurled their King from his throne and murdered him' (groans). 'They flung out of their country their ancient and famous nobility – they published the audacious doctrine of equality – they made a cadet of artillery, a beggarly lawyer's son, into an Emperor, and took ignoramuses from the ranks – drummers and privates, by Jove! – of whom they made kings, generals, and marshals! Is this to be borne?' (Cries of 'No! no!') 'Upon them, my boys! down with these godless revolutionists, and rally round the British lion!'

So saying, Ensign Snooks (whose flag, which he can't carry, is held by a huge grizzly color-sergeant) draws a little sword, and pipes out a feeble huzza. The men of his company, roaring curses at the Frenchmen, prepare to receive and repel a thundering charge of French cuirassiers. The men fight, and Snooks is knighted because the men fought so well.

But live or die, win or lose, what do *they* get? English glory is too genteel to meddle with those humble fellows. She does not condescend to ask the names of the poor devils whom she kills in her service. Why was not every private man's name written upon the stones in Waterloo Church as well as every officer's? Five hundred pounds to the stonecutters would have served to carve the whole catalogue, and paid the poor compliment of recognition to men who died in doing their duty. If the officers deserved a stone, the men did. But come, let us away and drop a tear over the Marquis of Anglesey's leg![14]

As for Waterloo, has it not been talked of enough after dinner? Here are some oats that were plucked before Hougoumont,[15] where grow not only oats, but flourishing crops of grape-shot, bayonets, and legion-of-honour crosses, in amazing profusion.

Well, though I made a vow not to talk about Waterloo either here or after dinner, there is one little secret admission that one must make after seeing it. Let an Englishman go and see that field, and he *never forgets it*. The sight is an event in his life; and, though it has been seen by millions of peaceable *gents* – grocers from Bond Street, meek attorneys from Chancery Lane, and timid tailors from Piccadilly – I will wager that there is not one of them but feels a glow as he looks at the place, and remembers that he, too, is an Englishman.

It is a wrong, egotistical, savage, unchristian feeling, and that's the truth of it. A man of peace has no right to be dazzled by that red-coated glory, and to intoxicate his vanity with those remembrances of carnage and triumph. The same sentence which tells us that on earth there ought to be peace and goodwill amongst men, tells us to whom GLORY belongs.

14. As recorded in Murray, the Marquis's amputated leg (he lived on, single-limbed) has a memorial tomb at Waterloo whereas thousands of Other Ranks are interred in unmarked graves.
15. Hougoumont was the name of a farmhouse, a site central in the battle. It was restored in 2015 for the bicentenary.

– The Court Circular –

Signed by 'Mr Snob' – from 'The Snobs of England'
in *Punch* (March 1847)

*The Court Circular was the diary of the previous day's
doings by royalty, their courtiers, and other people of
eminence. It was originated at the turn of the century by
George III, whose 'Court Newsman' released official,
and characteristically trivial, records to chosen newspapers. It continues today in* The Times *and* Telegraph.

*Thackeray's famous 'snobography' put into gen-
eral circulation a word generally thought to sum up
the primum mobile of English life. The peculiarity of
English snobbery, as Thackeray anatomised it, is that
you truckle slavishly to those above you – hoping for
advantage – and scorn those beneath you, keeping them
'in their place'.*

*English snobbery gives house-room to a host of
prejudices: xenophobia, anti-intellectualism, and the
abject worship of royalty, wealth and rank – even those
as degenerate as the Prince Regent George, or Prince
Albert (whom* Punch *hated at this period). In this paper
he is said to be disguised as a Portuguese Prince Consort.*

Thackeray borrowed the word 'snob'[1] *from un-
dergraduate slang at Cambridge in which townspeople
were divided into 'nobs and snobs': upper and lower
classes. It was G. K. Chesterton who paid Thackeray the*

1. The word had the street meaning 'cobbler'.

supreme compliment about the snob papers: 'Dickens, or Douglas Jerrold, or many others might have planned a Book of Snobs; it was Thackeray, and Thackeray alone, who wrote the great subtitle, "By One of Themselves".'

E xample is the best of precepts; so let us begin with a true and authentic story, showing how young aristocratic snobs are reared, and how early their Snobbishness may be made to bloom. A beautiful and fashionable lady – (pardon, gracious madam, that your story should be made public; but it is so moral that it ought to be known to the universal world) – told me that in her early youth she had a little acquaintance, who is now indeed a beautiful and fashionable lady too. In mentioning Miss Snobky, daughter of Sir Snobby Snobky, whose presentation at Court caused such a sensation, need I say more?

When Miss Snobky was so very young as to be in the nursery regions, and to walk off early mornings in St James's Park, protected by a French governess and followed by a huge hirsute flunkey[2] in the canary coloured livery of the Snobkys, she used occasionally in these promenades to meet with young Lord Claude Lollipop, the Marquis of Sillabub's younger son. In the very height of the season, from some unexplained cause, the Snobkys suddenly determined upon leaving town. Miss Snobky spoke to her female friend and confidante. 'What will poor Claude Lollipop say when he hears of my absence?' asked the tender-hearted child.

'Oh, perhaps he won't hear of it,' answers the confidante.

'*My dear, he will read it in the papers,*' replied the dear little fashionable rogue of seven years old. She

2. i.e., wig-wearing.

knew already her importance, and how all the world of England, how all the would-be-genteel people, how all the silver-fork worshippers, how all the tattle-mongers, how all the grocers' ladies, the tailors' ladies, the attorneys' and merchants' ladies, and the people living at Clapham and Brunswick Square, who have no more chance of consorting with a Snobky than my beloved reader has of dining with the Emperor of China – yet watched the movements of the Snobkys with interest and were glad to know when they came to London and left it.

Here is the account of Miss Snobky's dress, and that of her mother, Lady Snobky, from the papers: –

'MISS SNOBKY.

'*Habit de Cour*, composed of a yellow nankeen illusion dress over a slip of rich pea-green corduroy, trimmed *en tablier*, with bouquets of Brussels sprouts: the body and sleeves handsomely trimmed with calimanco, and festooned with a pink train and white radishes. Head dress, carrots and lappets.

'LADY SNOBKY.

'*Costume de Cour*, composed of a train of the most superb Pekin bandannas, elegantly trimmed with spangles, tinfoil, and red-tape. Bodice and underdress of sky-blue velveteen, trimmed with *bouffants* and *noeuds* of bell-pulls. Stomacher, a muffin. Head-dress, a bird's nest, with a bird of paradise, over a rich brass knocker *en ferronière*. This splendid costume, by Madame Crinoline, of Regent Street, was the object of universal admiration.'

This is what you read. Oh, Mrs Ellis![3] Oh, mothers, daughters, aunts, grandmothers of England, this is the sort of writing which is put in the newspapers for you! How can you help being the mothers, daughters, &c., of Snobs, so long as this balderdash is set before you?

You stuff the little rosy foot of a Chinese young lady of fashion into a slipper that is about the size of a salt-cruet, and keep the poor little toes there imprisoned and twisted up so long that the dwarfishness becomes irremediable. Later, the foot would not expand to the natural size were you to give her a washing-tub for a shoe and for all her life she has little feet, and is a cripple. O, my dear Miss Wiggins, thank your stars that those beautiful feet of yours – though I declare when you walk they are so small as to be almost invisible – thank your stars that society never so practised upon them; but look around and see how many friends of ours in the highest circles have had their *brains* so prematurely and hopelessly pinched and distorted.

How can you expect that those poor creatures are to move naturally when the world and their parents have mutilated them so cruelly? As long as a Court Circular exists, how the deuce are people whose names are chronicled in it ever to believe themselves

3. Mrs Ellis (Sarah Stickney Ellis) author of the pious conduct manuals: *The Wives of England* (1843), *The Women of England* (1839), *The Mothers of England* (1843), and *The Daughters of England* (1842). She is a frequent satirical target in *Punch*.

the equals of the cringing race which daily reads that abominable trash? I believe that ours is the only country in the world now where the Court Circular remains in full flourish – where you read, 'This day his Royal Highness Prince Pattypan was taken an airing in his go-cart.' 'The Princess Pimminy was taken a drive, attended by her ladies of honour, and accompanied by her doll,' &c. We laugh at the solemnity with which Saint Simon announces that *Sa Majesté se médicamente aujourd'hui*.[4] Under our very noses the same folly is daily going on. That wonderful and mysterious man, the author of the Court Circular, drops in with his budget at the newspaper offices every night. I once asked the Editor of a paper to allow me to lie in wait and see him.[5]

I am told that in a kingdom where there is a German King-Consort (Portugal it must be, for the Queen of that country married a German Prince, who is greatly admired and respected by the natives), whenever the Consort takes the diversion of shooting among the rabbit-warrens of Cintra, or the pheasant-preserve of Mafra, he has a keeper to load his guns, as a matter of course, and then they are handed to the nobleman, his equerry, and the nobleman hands them to the Prince who blazes away – gives back the discharged gun to the nobleman, who gives it to the

4. 'His majesty took some medicine today' – recorded the Duc de Saint Simon, slavish diarist of the banal at the court of Louis XIV.
5. The Court Newsman, a royal employee, see above.

keeper, and so on. But the Prince *won't take the gun from the hands of the loader.*[6]

As long as this unnatural and monstrous etiquette continues, Snobs there must be. The three persons engaged in this transaction are, for the time being, Snobs.

1. The keeper – the least Snob of all, because he is discharging his daily duty; but he appears here as a Snob, that is to say, in a position of debasement before another human being (the Prince), with whom he is allowed to communicate through another party. A free Portuguese gamekeeper, who professes himself to be unworthy to communicate directly with any person, confesses himself to be a Snob.

2. The nobleman in waiting is a Snob. If it degrades the Prince to receive the gun from the game-keeper, it is degrading to the nobleman in waiting to execute that service. He acts as a Snob towards the keeper, whom he keeps from communication with the Prince – a Snob to the Prince, to whom he pays a degrading homage.

3. The King-Consort of Portugal is a Snob for insulting fellow-men in this way. There's no harm in his accepting the services of the keeper directly; but indirectly he insults the service performed, and the servants who perform it; and therefore, I say, respectfully, is a most undoubted, though royal SN–B.

6. *Punch* and Thackeray were hostile to Albert, the German Prince Consort, and made mock of his non-English hunting practices. There were popular pictures of Albert pheasant and stag hunting with the retinue Mr Snob here describes.

And then you read in the *Diario do Goberno* – 'Yesterday his Majesty the King took the diversion of shooting the woods off Cintra, attended by Colonel the honourable Whiskerando Sombrero. His Majesty returned to the Necessidades to lunch, at,' &c., &c.

Oh! that Court Circular! once more, I exclaim. Down with the Court Circular – that engine and propagator of Snobbishness! I promise to subscribe for a year to any daily paper that shall come out without a Court Circular – were it the *Morning Herald*[7] itself. When I read that trash, I rise in my wrath; I feel myself disloyal, a regicide, a member of the Calf's Head Club.[8] The only Court Circular story which ever pleased me, was that of the King of Spain, who in great part was roasted, because there was not time for the Prime Minister to command the Lord Chamberlain to desire the Grand Gold Stick to order the first page in waiting to bid the chief of the flunkeys to request the Housemaid of Honour to bring up a pail of water to put his Majesty out.

I am like the Pasha of three tails,[9] to whom the Sultan sends *his* Court Circular, the bowstring.

It *chokes* me. May its usage be abolished for ever!

7. A Tory newspaper, sworn foe of radical *Punch*.
8. The secretive Calves' (or Calf's) Head Club was set up after the execution, by axe, of Charles I. It had rituals (including a ceremonial decapitated calf's head) urging republican ideals and the downfall of monarchic tyranny.
9. The pasha of three pig tails was beneath the Sultan (alone permitted four tails), vice-regal, and permitted to order execution. Thackeray had picked up much lore about the Orient in his travelogue titled *Notes of a Journey from Cornhill to Grand Cairo* (1846).

– Before the Curtain –

Signed William Makepeace Thackeray. The appended preface to the second edition of *Vanity Fair* (1848)

This preface to Vanity Fair *was published after the novel's highly successful monthly serial came to its end. It was printed in the volume edition.*

As the manager of the Performance sits before the curtain on the boards and looks into the Fair, a feeling of profound melancholy comes over him in his survey of the bustling place. There is a great quantity of eating and drinking, making love and jilting, laughing and the contrary, smoking, cheating, fighting, dancing and fiddling; there are bullies pushing about, bucks ogling the women, knaves picking pockets, policemen on the look-out, quacks (*other* quacks, plague take them!) bawling in front of their booths, and yokels looking up at the tinselled dancers and poor old rouged tumblers, while the light-fingered folk are operating upon their pockets behind. Yes, this is *Vanity Fair*;[1] not a moral place certainly; nor a merry one,

---

1. Thackeray's title was taken from John Bunyan's *The Pilgrim's Progress* where 'Vanity Fair' – London – is a mortal threat to the Christian soul. Thackeray is more tolerant of the Great Wen.

though very noisy. Look at the faces of the actors and buffoons when they come off from their business; and Tom Fool washing the paint off his cheeks before he sits down to dinner with his wife and the little Jack Puddings behind the canvas. The curtain will be up presently, and he will be turning over head and heels, and crying, 'How are you?'

A man with a reflective turn of mind, walking through an exhibition of this sort, will not be oppressed, I take it, by his own or other people's hilarity. An episode of humour or kindness touches and amuses him here and there – a pretty child looking at a gingerbread stall; a pretty girl blushing whilst her lover talks to her and chooses her fairing; poor Tom Fool, yonder behind the waggon, mumbling his bone with the honest family which lives by his tumbling; but the general impression is one more melancholy than mirthful. When you come home you sit down in a sober, contemplative, not uncharitable frame of mind, and apply yourself to your books or your business.

I have no other moral than this to tag to the present story of 'Vanity Fair'. Some people consider Fairs immoral altogether, and eschew such, with their servants and families: very likely they are right. But persons who think otherwise, and are of a lazy, or a benevolent, or a sarcastic mood, may perhaps like to step in for half an hour, and look at the performances. There are scenes of all sorts; some dreadful combats, some grand and lofty horse-riding, some scenes of high life, and some of very middling indeed; some love-making for the sentimental, and some light comic business; the whole accompanied by appropriate scenery and brilliantly illuminated with the Author's own candles.[2]

What more has the Manager of the Performance to say? – To acknowledge the kindness with which it has been received in all the principal towns of England through which the Show has passed, and where it has been most favourably noticed by the respected conductors of the public Press, and by the Nobility and Gentry. He is proud to think that his Puppets have given satisfaction to the very best company in this empire. The famous little Becky Puppet has been pronounced to be uncommonly flexible in the joints, and lively on the wire; the Amelia Doll, though it has had a smaller circle of admirers, has yet been carved and dressed with the greatest care by the artist; the Dobbin Figure, though apparently clumsy, yet dances in a very amusing and natural manner; the Little Boys' Dance has been liked by some; and please to remark the richly dressed figure of the Wicked Nobleman, on which no expense has been spared, and which Old Nick will fetch away at the end of this singular performance.

And with this, and a profound bow to his patrons, the Manager retires, and the curtain rises.

LONDON, June 28, 1848

2. Thackeray alludes to his own illustrations to the novel.

– Frontispiece Illustration
for *Vanity Fair* –

(1848)

For the volume edition, after Vanity Fair's *nineteen-month serial run, Thackeray added this pregnant frontispiece. The clown, Harlequin – a member of a travelling troupe described in 'Before the Curtain' – looks at himself sadly in a cracked mirror. A coffin-like box is behind him. One of the dolls (the unsinkable Becky Sharp, one assumes) is uncoffined.*

A cross (the parson's badge of office) lies unused alongside him. In the background is the church of Ottery St Mary, the Devon village where Thackeray was happiest as a child.

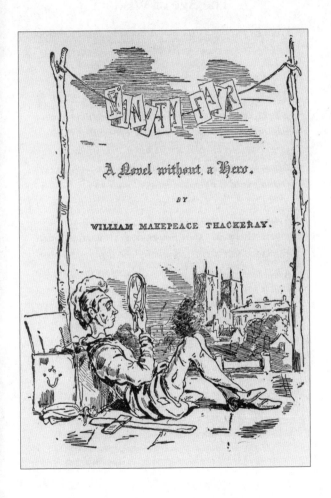

– The Age of Wisdom –

From *Rebecca and Rowena: A Romance upon Romance*
(1851)

Thackeray reached forty in 1851 – a year in which he was at the climax of his fame, while writing Henry Esmond. *It was also a period of his greatest personal wretchedness. He was unhappily married to a woman whom he could not divorce. He fell in love with his best friend's wife. It provoked misery for all.*

This ballad is by a man who has, as he says in Vanity Fair, *'lived and loved' – and not found happiness.* Rebecca and Rowena: A Romance upon Romance *was a satirical fantasy about the main characters in Scott's novel* Ivanhoe. *Thackeray imagines the couple's romantic love souring in their middle age.*

The title of this world-weary ballad was prominently quoted by Dickens in the famous overture to A Tale of Two Cities *(1859): 'It was the best of times, it was the worst of times, it was the age of wisdom, it was the age of foolishness . . .'*

Ho, pretty page, with the dimpled chin,
That never has known the Barber's shear,
All your wish is woman to win,
This is the way that boys begin, –

Wait till you come to Forty Year.
Curly gold locks cover foolish brains,
Billing and cooing is all your cheer;
Sighing and singing of midnight strains,
Under Bonnybell's window panes, –

Wait till you come to Forty Year.
Forty times over let Michaelmas pass,
Grizzling hair the brain doth clear –
Then you know a boy is an ass,
Then you know the worth of a lass,
Once you have come to Forty Year.

Pledge me round, I bid ye declare,
All good fellows whose beards are grey,
Did not the fairest of the fair
Common grow and wearisome ere
Ever a month was passed away?

The reddest lips that ever have kissed,
The brightest eyes that ever have shone,
May pray and whisper, and we not list,
Or look away, and never be missed,
Ere yet ever a month is gone.

Gillian's dead, God rest her bier,
How I loved her twenty years syne!
Marian's married, but I sit here
Alone and merry at Forty Year,
Dipping my nose in the Gascon wine.

– The Death of Colonel Newcome –

From *The Newcomes* – 'Edited by Arthur Pendennis'
(1856)

*Anthony Trollope eulogised Colonel Newcome, the
English gentleman whom he felt 'has no equal in
English fiction'.*

*Thackeray's old school Charterhouse (renamed
here 'Grey Friars') has almshouses for forty or more
former pupils who have fallen on hard times. The ruined Colonel Newcome finds refuge as a brother. His
last word, as the school bell tolls the start of lessons, is
'Adsum'. I am here. Then he is here no more. It is the second most famous death scene in Victorian fiction – and
unlike that of Little Nell, has a wealth of social depth
to it. Holly Furneaux makes the point in an authorita-
tive essay on the importance of Colonel Newcome in
Victorian social ideology.[1] His idealised image persisted
into Edwardian England – there were dramatic adapta-
tions, notably one in 1906 with the eminent Beerbohm
Tree playing the Colonel for ten years, on and off. The
death-scene was, inevitably, the dramatic climax. It all
fed into a powerful notion of the warrior gentleman.
Many young officers, one may fantasise, died in the
Great War with the word 'adsum' on their lips or in
their hearts.*

1. *The Oxford Handbook of Victorian Literary Culture* (2016), ed Juliet
John, Chapter 11, 'Victorian Masculinities'.

C live, and the boy sometimes with him, used to go daily to Grey Friars, where the Colonel still lay ill. After some days the fever which had attacked him left him, but left him so weak and enfeebled that he could only go from his bed to the chair by his fireside. The season was exceedingly bitter, the chamber which he inhabited was warm and spacious; it was considered unadvisable to move him until he had attained greater strength, and till warmer weather. The medical men of the House hoped he might rally in spring. My friend, Dr Goodenough, came to him; he hoped too: but not with a hopeful face. A chamber, luckily vacant, hard by the Colonel's, was assigned to his friends, where we sate when we were too many for him. Besides his customary attendant, he had two dear and watchful nurses, who were almost always with him – Ethel and Madame de Florac, who had passed many a faithful year by an old man's bedside; who would have come, as to a work of religion, to any sick couch, much more to this one, where he lay for whose life she would once gladly have given her own.

But our Colonel, we all were obliged to acknowledge, was no more our friend of old days. He knew us again, and was good to every one round him, as his wont was; especially when Boy came, his old eyes lighted up with simple happiness, and, with eager trembling hands, he would seek under his bedclothes, or the pockets of his dressing-gown, for toys or cakes, which he had caused to be purchased for his grandson. There was a little laughing, red-cheeked, white-headed gown-boy of the school, to whom the old man had taken a great fancy. One of the symptoms of his returning consciousness and recovery, as we hoped, was his calling for this child, who pleased our friend by his archness and merry ways; and who, to the old gentleman's unfailing delight, used to call him, 'Codd Colonel'. 'Tell little F—, that Codd Colonel wants to see him;' and the little gown-boy was brought to him; and the Colonel would listen to him for hours; and hear all about his lessons and his play; and prattle almost as childishly about Dr Raine,[2] and his own early school-days. The boys of the school, it must be said, had heard the noble old gentleman's touching history, and had all got to know and love him. They came every day to hear news of him; sent him in books and papers to amuse him; and some benevolent young souls, – God's blessing on all honest boys, say I, – painted theatrical characters, and sent them in to Codd Colonel's grandson. The little fellow was made free of gown-boys, and once came thence to his grandfather in a little gown, which delighted the old man hugely. Boy said he would like to be a little gown-boy; and I make no doubt, when he is old enough, his father will get him that post, and put him under the tuition of my friend Dr Senior.

So, weeks passed away, during which our dear

2. Matthew Raine was the headmaster at Charterhouse from 1791 to 1811.

old friend still remained with us. His mind was gone at intervals, but would rally feebly; and with his consciousness returned his love, his simplicity, his sweetness. He would talk French with Madame de Florac, at which time, his memory appeared to awaken with surprising vividness, his cheek flushed, and he was a youth again, – a youth all love and hope, – a stricken old man, with a beard as white as snow covering the noble careworn face. At such times he called her by her Christian name of Léonore;[3] he addressed courtly old words of regard and kindness to the aged lady; anon he wandered in his talk, and spoke to her as if they still were young. Now, as in those early days, his heart was pure; no anger remained in it; no guile tainted it; only peace and good-will dwelt in it.

Rosey's death had seemed to shock him for a while when the unconscious little boy spoke of it. Before that circumstance, Clive had even forbore to wear mourning, lest the news should agitate his father. The Colonel remained silent and was very much disturbed all that day, but he never appeared to comprehend the fact quite; and, once or twice afterwards, asked, why she did not come to see him? She was prevented, he supposed – she was prevented, he said, with a look of terror: he never once otherwise alluded to that unlucky tyrant of his household, who had made his last

3. Léonore was the woman the Colonel loved in his youth but never married, as Clive loved but could never marry Ethel. Rosey is Clive's wife, whom he loved less.

years so unhappy.[4]

The circumstance of Clive's legacy he never understood: but more than once spoke of Barnes to Ethel, and sent his compliments to him, and said he should like to shake him by the hand. Barnes Newcome never once offered to touch that honoured hand, though his sister bore her uncle's message to him. They came often from Bryanstone Square; Mrs Hobson even offered to sit with the Colonel, and read to him, and brought him books for his improvement. But her presence disturbed him; he cared not for her books; the two nurses whom he loved faithfully watched him; and my wife and I were admitted to him sometimes, both of whom he honoured with regard and recognition. As for F. B.,[5] in order to be near his Colonel, did not that good fellow take up his lodging in Cistercian Lane, at the 'Red Cow'? He is one whose errors, let us hope, shall be pardoned, *quia multum amavit*.[6] I am sure he felt ten times more joy at hearing of Clive's legacy, than if thousands had been bequeathed to himself. May good health and good fortune speed him!

The days went on, and our hopes, raised sometimes, began to flicker and fail. One evening the Colonel left

4. Rosey's mother, the 'Old Campaigner', who made the Colonel's life miserable when destitution forced him to lodge with her. She is modelled on Thackeray's mother-in-law, who blamed him for her daughter's madness.
5. Fred Bayham, a good-natured barrister, down on his luck, who smuggles in good things to the Colonel.
6. Because he loved him greatly.

his chair for his bed in pretty good spirits, but passed a disturbed night, and the next morning was too weak to rise. Then he remained in his bed, and his friends visited him there. One afternoon he asked for his little gown-boy, and the child was brought to him, and sate by the bed with a very awestricken face; and then gathered courage, and tried to amuse him by telling him how it was a half-holiday, and they were having a cricket-match with the St Peter's boys in the green, and Grey Friars was in and winning. The Colonel quite understood about it; he would like to see the game; he had played many a game on that green when he was a boy. He grew excited; Clive dismissed his father's little friend, and put a sovereign into his hand; and away he ran to say that Codd Colonel had come into a fortune, and to buy tarts, and to see the match out. *I, curre,*[7] little white-haired gown-boy! Heaven speed you, little friend!

After the child had gone, Thomas Newcome began to wander more and more. He talked louder; he gave the word of command, spoke Hindustanee as if to his men. Then he spoke words in French rapidly, seizing a hand that was near him and crying, 'Toujours, toujours!' But it was Ethel's hand which he took. Ethel and Clive and the nurse were in the room with him; the latter came to us, who were sitting in the adjoining apartment; Madame de Florac was there, with my wife and Bayham.

At the look in the woman's countenance Madame

7. Run!

de Florac started up. 'He is very bad, he wanders a great deal,' the nurse whispered. The French lady fell instantly on her knees, and remained rigid in prayer.

Some time afterwards Ethel came in with a scared face to our pale group. 'He is calling for you again, dear lady,' she said, going up to Madame de Florac, who was still kneeling; 'and just now he said he wanted Pendennis to take care of his boy. He will not know you.' She hid her tears as she spoke.

She went into the room, where Clive was at the bed's foot; the old man within it talked on rapidly for a while: then again he would sigh and be still: once more I heard him say hurriedly, 'Take care of him while I'm in India;' and then with a heart-rending voice he called out, 'Léonore, Léonore!' She was kneeling by his side now. The patient's voice sank into faint murmurs; only a moan now and then announced that he was not asleep.

At the usual evening hour the chapel bell began to toll, and Thomas Newcome's hands outside the bed feebly beat a time. And just as the last bell struck, a peculiar sweet smile shone over his face, and he lifted up his head a little, and quickly said, 'Adsum!'[8] and fell back. It was the word we used at school, when names were called; and lo, he, whose heart was as that of a little child, had answered to his name, and stood in the presence of The Master.

8. 'I am present.'

– On Two Children in Black –

Signed 'Mr Roundabout' – from *The Roundabout Papers*
(March 1860)

First published in the Cornhill Magazine, *shortly after
Thackeray's taking over the editorship, March 1860.*

*Mr Roundabout was the last, and in many ways
the most Thackerayan of Thackeray's pseudonyms and
personae. Roundabout was created for a series of essays
Thackeray wrote as editor for* Cornhill – *the sumptuous
monthly magazine created by George Smith in 1860.*

*The appeal of the essays, and their crowning posi-
tion in Thackeray's non-fictional oeuvre, is described by
Gordon Ray: 'Of all forms, indeed, the familiar essay
was best adapted to the Thackeray of these years, who
possessed a mind full but tired and a style capable of
making the most trivial subject interesting. Certainly his*
Roundabouts *were the only part of his later work that
he actively enjoyed composing . . . No literary form is
more out of favour today than the familiar essay. Should
a taste for it revive, the* Roundabout Papers *may, once
again, enjoy the wide popularity that was theirs during
the fifty years after their first publication, for they are
classics of their kind.'*[1]

1. Gordon N. Ray, *The Age of Wisdom* (1958).

Montaigne and 'Howel's Letters' are my bedside books.[2] If I wake at night, I have one or other of them to prattle me to sleep again. They talk about themselves for ever, and don't weary me. I like to hear them tell their old stories over and over again. I read them in the dozy hours, and only half remember them. I am informed that both of them tell coarse stories. I don't heed them. It was the custom of their time, as it is of Highlanders and Hottentots to dispense with a part of dress which we all wear in cities. But people can't afford to be shocked either at Cape Town or at Inverness every time they meet an individual who wears his national airy raiment. I never knew the 'Arabian Nights' was an improper book until I happened once to read it in a 'family edition'. Well, *qui s'excuse* . . . Who, pray, has accused me as yet? Here am I smothering dear good old Mrs Grundy's[3] objections, before she has opened her mouth. I love, I say, and scarcely ever tire of hearing, the artless prattle of those two dear old friends, the Perigourdin gentleman and the priggish little Clerk of King Charles's Council.[4] Their egotism in nowise disgusts me. I hope I shall always like to hear

2. Montaigne's essays and James Howel(l)'s (1599–1666) 'familiar letters': both are influential on Thackeray's own 'familiar essay'. The auction of his books, after his death, confirmed he had both volumes.
3. Mrs Grundy was the mythical incarnation of Victorian censoriousness – the insistence that nothing be put into print that might bring a blush to a maiden's cheek.
4. Montaigne lived in a château near Périgord. Howell was employed, briefly, as a secretary to Charles the first's Privy Council.

men, in reason, talk about themselves. What subject does a man know better? If I stamp on a friend's corn, his outcry is genuine – he confounds my clumsiness in the accents of truth. He is speaking about himself and expressing his emotion of grief or pain in a manner perfectly authentic and veracious. I have a story of my own, of a wrong done to me by somebody, as far back as the year 1838: whenever I think of it and have had a couple of glasses of wine, I *cannot* help telling it. The toe is stamped upon; the pain is just as keen as ever: I cry out, and perhaps utter imprecatory language. I told the story only last Wednesday at dinner: –

'Mr Roundabout,' says a lady sitting by me, 'how comes it that in your books there is a certain class (it may be of men, or it may be of women, but that is not the question in point) – how comes it, dear sir, there is a certain class of persons whom you always attack in your writings, and savagely rush at, goad, poke, toss up in the air, kick, and trample on?'

I couldn't help myself. I knew I ought not to do it. I told her the whole story, between the *entrées* and the roast. The wound began to bleed again. The horrid pang was there, as keen and as fresh as ever. If I live half as long as Tithonus,[5] that crack across my heart can never be cured. There are wrongs and griefs that

5. Tennyson's poem about the mythical character Tithonus, who is doomed never to die (but not given eternal youth), was published in the previous issue of the *Cornhill Magazine*. It created a considerable stir.

can't be mended. It is all very well of you, my dear Mrs G., to say that this spirit is unchristian, and that we ought to forgive and forget, and so forth. How can I forget at will? How forgive? I can forgive the occasional waiter who broke my beautiful old decanter at that very dinner. I am not going to do him any injury. But all the powers on earth can't make that claret-jug whole.

So, you see, I told the lady the inevitable story. I was egotistical. I was selfish, no doubt; but I was natural, and was telling the truth. You say you are angry with a man for talking about himself. It is because you yourself are selfish, that that other person's Self does not interest you. Be interested by other people and with their affairs. Let them prattle and talk to you, as I do my dear old egotists just mentioned. When you have had enough of them, and sudden hazes come over your eyes, lay down the volume; pop out the candle, and *dormez bien*.[6] I should like to write a nightcap book – a book that you can muse over, that you can smile over, that you can yawn over – a book of which you can say, 'Well, this man is so and so and so and so; but he has a friendly heart (although some wiseacres have painted him as black as bogey), and you may trust what he says.' I should like to touch you sometimes with a reminiscence that shall waken your sympathy, and make you say, *Io anchè*[7] have so thought, felt,

6. Sleep well.
7. I also (Italian).

smiled, suffered. Now, how is this to be done except by egotism? *Linea recta brevissima.*[8] That right line 'I' is the very shortest, simplest, straightforwardest means of communication between us, and stands for what it is worth and no more. Sometimes authors say, 'The present writer has often remarked;' or 'The undersigned has observed;' or 'Mr Roundabout presents his compliments to the gentle reader, and begs to state,' &c.: but 'I' is better and straighter than all these grimaces of modesty: and although these are Roundabout Papers, and may wander who knows whither, I shall ask leave to maintain the upright and simple perpendicular. When this bundle of egotisms is bound up together, as they may be one day, if no accident prevents this tongue from wagging, or this ink from running, they will bore you very likely; so it would to read through 'Howel's Letters' from beginning to end, or to eat up the whole of a ham; but a slice on occasion may have a relish: a dip into the volume at random and so on for a page or two: and now and then a smile; and presently a gape; and the book drops out of your hand; and so, *bon soir*, and pleasant dreams to you. I have frequently seen men at clubs asleep over their humble servant's works, and am always pleased. Even at a lecture I don't mind, if they don't snore. Only the other day when my friend A. said, 'You've left off that Roundabout business, I see; very glad you have,' I joined in the general

8. A straight line is the shortest distance.

roar of laughter at the table. I don't care a fig whether Archilochus[9] likes the papers or no. You don't like partridge, Archilochus, or porridge, or what not? Try some other dish. I am not going to force mine down your throat, or quarrel with you if you refuse it. Once in America a clever and candid woman said to me, at the close of a dinner, during which I had been sitting beside her, 'Mr Roundabout, I was told I should not like you; and I don't.' 'Well, ma'am,' says I, in a tone of the most unfeigned simplicity, 'I don't care.' And we became good friends immediately, and esteemed each other ever after.

So, my dear Archilochus, if you come upon this paper, and say, 'Fudge!' and pass on to another, I for one shall not be in the least mortified. If you say, 'What does he mean by calling this paper "On Two Children in Black", when there's nothing about people in black at all, unless the ladies he met (and evidently bored) at dinner, were black women? What is all this egotistical pother? A plague on his I's!' My dear fellow, if you read 'Montaigne's Essays', you must own that he might call almost any one by the name of any other, and that an essay on the Moon or an essay on Green Cheese would be as appropriate a title as one of his on Coaches, on the Art of Discoursing, or Experience, or what you will. Besides, if I *have* a subject (and I have) I claim to approach it in a roundabout manner.

9. Archilochus, an ancient Greek poet, famed for his egotism and his savage invective.

You remember Balzac's tale of the 'Peau de Chagrin',[10] and how every time the possessor used it for the accomplishment of some wish the fairy *peau* shrank a little and the owner's life correspondingly shortened? I have such a desire to be well with my public that I am actually giving up my favourite story. I am killing my goose, I know I am. I can't tell my story of the children in black after this; after printing it, and sending it through the country. When they are gone to the printer's these little things become public property. I take their hands. I bless them. I say, 'Good-bye, my little dears.' I am quite sorry to part with them: but the fact is, I have told all my friends about them already, and don't dare to take them about with me any more.

Now every word is true of this little anecdote, and I submit that there lies in it a most curious and exciting little mystery. I am like a man who gives you the last bottle of his '25 claret. It is the pride of his cellar; he knows it, and he has a right to praise it. He takes up the bottle, fashioned so slenderly – takes it up tenderly, cants it with care, places it before his friends, declares how good it is, with honest pride, and wishes he had a hundred dozen bottles more of the same wine in his cellar. *Si quid novisti*, &c.,[11] I shall be very glad to hear

10. *La Peau de Chagrin* (1831). Honoré de Balzac's title is hard to translate. The standard English versions *The Skin of Sorrow* and *The Wild Ass's Skin* are both unsatisfactory. Thackeray was influenced by Balzac's panoramic social novels.
11. From Thackeray's beloved Horace: loosely 'if you can tell something better, let me know.'

from you. I protest and vow I am giving you the best I have.

Well, who those little boys in black were, I shall never probably know to my dying day. They were very pretty little men, with pale faces, and large, melancholy eyes; and they had beautiful little hands, and little boots, and the finest little shirts, and black paletots[12] lined with the richest silk; and they had picture-books in several languages, English, and French, and German, I remember. Two more aristocratic-looking little men I never set eyes on. They were travelling with a very handsome, pale lady in mourning, and a maid-servant dressed in black, too; and on the lady's face there was the deepest grief. The little boys clambered and played about the carriage, and she sat watching. It was a railway-carriage from Frankfort to Heidelberg.[13]

I saw at once that she was the mother of those children, and going to part from them. Perhaps I have tried parting with my own, and not found the business very pleasant. Perhaps I recollect driving down (with a certain trunk and carpet-bag on the box) with my own mother to the end of the avenue, where we waited – only a few minutes – until the whirring wheels of that 'Defiance' coach[14] were heard rolling towards us

12. Overcoats. Black, because the family is in mourning.
13. Thackeray gives no precise dates. But it is safe to assume this event occurred on the long Continental tour he undertook with his daughters in 1853.
14. In the pre-railway age the 'Defiance' coach carried passengers from London to the Midlands and the north of England.

as certain as death. Twang goes the horn; up goes the trunk; down come the steps. Bah! I see the autumn evening: I hear the wheels now: I smart the cruel smart again: and, boy or man, have never been able to bear the sight of people parting from their children.

I thought these little men might be going to school for the first time in their lives; and mamma might be taking them to the Doctor, and would leave them with many fond charges, and little wistful secrets of love, bidding the elder to protect his younger brother, and the younger to be gentle, and to remember to pray to God always for his mother, who would pray for her boy too. Our party made friends with these young ones during the little journey; but the poor lady was too sad to talk except to the boys now and again, and sat in her corner, pale, and silently looking at them.

The next day, we saw the lady and her maid driving in the direction of the railway-station, *without the boys.* The parting had taken place, then. That night they would sleep among strangers. The little beds at home were vacant, and poor mother might go and look at them. Well, tears flow, and friends part, and mothers pray every night all over the world. I dare say we went to see Heidelberg Castle, and admired the vast shattered walls and quaint gables; and the Neckar running its bright course through that charming scene of peace and beauty; and ate our dinner, and drank our wine with relish. The poor mother would eat but little

Abendessen[15] that night; and, as for the children – that first night at school – hard bed, hard words, strange boys bullying, and laughing, and jarring you with their hateful merriment – as for the first night at a strange school, we most of us remember what *that* is. And the first is not the *worst*, my boys, there's the rub. But each man has his share of troubles, and, I suppose, you must have yours.

From Heidelberg we went to Baden-Baden: and, I dare say, saw Madame de Schlangenbad and Madame de la Cruchecassee, and Count Punter, and honest Captain Blackball. And whom should we see in the evening, but our two little boys, walking on each side of a fierce, yellow-faced, bearded man! We wanted to renew our acquaintance with them, and they were coming forward quite pleased to greet us. But the father pulled back one of the little men by his paletot, gave a grim scowl, and walked away. I can see the children now looking rather frightened away from us and up into the father's face, or the cruel uncle's – which was he? I think he was the father. So this was the end of them. Not school, as I at first had imagined. The mother was gone, who had given them the heaps of pretty books, and the pretty studs in the shirts, and the pretty silken clothes, and the tender – tender cares; and they were handed to this scowling practitioner of Trente et Quarante.[16] Ah! this is

15. Supper.
16. A card game popular in continental casinos, known in England as Red and Black.

worse than school. Poor little men! poor mother sitting by the vacant little beds! We saw the children once or twice after, always in Scowler's company; but we did not dare to give each other any marks of recognition.

From Baden we went to Basle, and thence to Lucerne, and so over the St Gothard into Italy. From Milan we went to Venice; and now comes the singular part of my story. In Venice there is a little court of which I forget the name: but in it is an apothecary's shop, whither I went to buy some remedy for the bites of certain animals which abound in Venice. Crawling animals, skipping animals, and humming, flying animals; all three will have at you at once; and one night nearly drove me into a strait-waistcoat. Well, as I was coming out of the apothecary's with the bottle of spirits of hartshorn in my hand (it really does do the bites a great deal of good), whom should I light upon but one of my little Heidelberg-Baden boys!

I have said how handsomely they were dressed as long as they were with their mother. When I saw the boy at Venice, who perfectly recognised me, his only garb was a wretched yellow cotton gown. His little feet, on which I had admired the little shiny boots, were *without shoe or stocking*. He looked at me, ran to an old hag of a woman, who seized his hand; and with her he disappeared down one of the thronged lanes of the city.

From Venice we went to Trieste (the Vienna railway at that time was only opened as far as Laybach, and the magnificent Semmering Pass was not quite completed).[17] At a station between Laybach and Graetz, one of my companions alighted for refreshment, and came back to the carriage saying: –

'There's that horrible man from Baden, with the two little boys.'

Of course, we had talked about the appearance of the little boy at Venice, and his strange altered garb. My companion said they were pale, wretched-looking and *dressed quite shabbily.*

I got out at several stations, and looked at all the carriages. I could not see my little men. From that day to this I have never set eyes on them. That is all my story. Who were they? What could they be? How can you explain that mystery of the mother giving them up; of the remarkable splendour and elegance of their appearance while under her care; of their barefooted squalor in Venice, a month afterwards; of their shabby habiliments at Laybach? Had the father gambled away his money, and sold their clothes? How came they to have passed out of the hands of a refined lady (as she evidently was, with whom I first saw them) into the charge of quite a common woman like her with whom I saw one of the boys at Venice? Here is but one chapter of the story. Can any man write the next, or that preceding the strange one on which I happened to light? Who knows? the mystery may have some

17. The Semmering Pass across the Alps was completed in 1854, the year after the Thackerays' trip.

quite simple solution. I saw two children, attired like little princes, taken from their mother and consigned to other care; and a fortnight afterwards, one of them barefooted and like a beggar. Who will read this riddle of The Two Children in Black?

– De Finibus –

Signed 'Mr Roundabout' – from *The Roundabout Papers*
(August 1862)

De Finibus *('About Last Things') was published in the*
Cornhill Magazine *sixteen months before Thackeray's
death. He feels it coming.*

When Swift was in love with Stella, and despatch-
ing her a letter from London thrice a month by
the Irish packet, you may remember how he would begin letter No. xxiii., we will say, on the very day when
xxii. had been sent away, stealing out of the coffee-
house or the assembly so as to be able to prattle with
his dear; 'never letting go her kind hand, as it were,'
as some commentator or other has said in speaking of
the Dean and his amour.[1] When Mr Johnson, walking
to Dodsley's,[2] and touching the posts in Pall Mall as
he walked, forgot to pat the head of one of them, he
went back and imposed his hands on it, – impelled I

1. Jonathan Swift, the Dean of St Patrick's Anglican Cathedral in
Dublin, sustained an epistolary affair with 'Stella' (Esther Johnson)
whom he had known since her childhood. They may have been
secretly married.
2. Robert Dodsley's bookshop. Boswell narrates this eccentric practice of Samuel Johnson and the lamp-posts he passed on his walk.

know not by what superstition. I have this I hope not dangerous mania too. As soon as a piece of work is out of hand, and before going to sleep, I like to begin another: it may be to write only half a dozen lines: but that is something towards Number the Next. The printer's boy has not yet reached Green Arbour Court[3] with the copy. Those people who were alive half an hour since, Pendennis, Clive Newcome, and (what do you call him? What was the name of the last hero? I remember now!) Philip Firmin, have hardly drunk their glass of wine, and the mammas have only this minute got the children's cloaks on, and have been bowed out of my premises – and here I come back to the study again: *tamen usque recurro*.[4] How lonely it looks now all these people are gone! My dear good friends, some folks are utterly tired of you, and say, 'What a poverty of friends the man has! He is always asking us to meet those Pendennises, Newcomes, and so forth. Why does he not introduce us to some new characters? Why is he not thrilling like Twostars, learned and profound like Threestars, exquisitely humorous and human like Fourstars? Why, finally, is he not somebody else?' My good people, it is not only impossible to please you all, but it is absurd to try. The dish which one man devours, another dislikes. Is the dinner of to-day not to

3. Alongside Salisbury Square in the City of London where there was a cluster of printing shops.
4. Part quotation meaning: 'you may drive nature out with a pitchfork, but she will keep coming back.'

your taste? Let us hope to-morrow's entertainment will be more agreeable . . . I resume my original subject. What an odd, pleasant, humorous, melancholy feeling it is to sit in the study, alone and quiet, now all these people are gone who have been boarding and lodging with me for twenty months![5] They have interrupted my rest: they have plagued me at all sorts of minutes: they have thrust themselves upon me when I was ill, or wished to be idle, and I have growled out a 'Be hanged to you, can't you leave me alone now?' Once or twice they have prevented my going out to dinner. Many and many a time they have prevented my coming home, because I knew they were there waiting in the study, and a plague take them! and I have left home and family, and gone to dine at the Club, and told nobody where I went. They have bored me, those people. They have plagued me at all sorts of uncomfortable hours. They have made such a disturbance in my mind and house, that sometimes I have hardly known what was going on in my family, and scarcely have heard what my neighbour said to me. They are gone at last; and you would expect me to be at ease? Far from it. I should almost be glad if Woolcomb[6] would walk in and talk to me; or Twysden[7] reappear, take his place in that chair

---

5. The normal run of one of the full-length serial novels Thackeray has been talking about was twenty months.
6. The villain in *Philip*, Thackeray's last complete novel. His depiction of Woolcomb's mixed race, and name, is grating for modern readers.
7. Talbot Twysden, a pompous civil servant in *Philip*, distantly related to the hero.

opposite me, and begin one of his tremendous stories.

Madmen, you know, see visions, hold conversations with, even draw the likeness of, people invisible to you and me. Is this making of people out of fancy madness? and are novel-writers at all entitled to strait-waistcoats? I often forget people's names in life; and in my own stories contritely own that I make dreadful blunders regarding them; but I declare, my dear sir, with respect to the personages introduced into your humble servant's fables, I know the people utterly – I know the sound of their voices. A gentleman came in to see me the other day, who was so like the picture of Philip Firmin in Mr Walker's charming drawings in the *Cornhill Magazine*,[8] that he was quite a curiosity to me. The same eyes, beard, shoulders, just as you have seen them from month to month. Well, he is not like the Philip Firmin in my mind. Asleep, asleep in the grave, lies the bold, the generous, the reckless, the tender-hearted creature whom I have made to pass through those adventures which have just been brought to an end. It is years since I heard the laughter ringing, or saw the bright blue eyes. When I knew him both were young. I become young as I think of him. And this morning he was alive again in this room, ready to laugh, to fight, to weep. As I write, do you know, it is the grey of evening; the house is quiet;

8. Thackeray recruited Frederick Walker to do the illustrations for *Philip*, his last complete novel, in the realistic, near photographic style preferred for 'muscular fiction' of the 1860s.

everybody is out; the room is getting a little dark, and I look rather wistfully up from the paper with perhaps ever so little fancy that HE MAY COME IN. – No? No movement. No grey shade, growing more palpable, out of which at last look the well-known eyes. No, the printer came and took him away with the last page of the proofs. And with the printer's boy did the whole cortege of ghosts flit away, invisible? Ha! stay! What is this? Angels and ministers of grace![9] The door opens, and a dark form – enters, bearing a black – a black suit of clothes. It is John. He says it is time to dress for dinner.

—

Every man who has had his German tutor, and has been coached through the famous 'Faust' of Goethe (thou wert my instructor, good old Weissenborn, and these eyes beheld the great master himself in dear little Weimar town!)[10] has read those charming verses which are prefixed to the drama, in which the poet reverts to the time when his work was first composed, and recalls the friends now departed, who once listened to his song. The dear shadows rise up around him, he says; he lives in the past again. It is to-day which appears

9. Hamlet's exclamation (finishing 'defend us') on first meeting the ghost of his father on the Elsinore battlements.
10. In 1830, after his unsuccessful university career, Thackeray was sent to Weimar to further his education. There he was, indeed, taught by Herr Weissenborn and did have audiences with Goethe.

vague and visionary. We humbler writers cannot create Fausts, or raise up monumental works that shall endure for all ages; but our books are diaries, in which our own feelings must of necessity be set down. As we look to the page written last month, or ten years ago, we remember the day and its events; the child ill, mayhap, in the adjoining room, and the doubts and fears which racked the brain as it still pursued its work; the dear old friend who read the commencement of the tale, and whose gentle hand shall be laid in ours no more. I own for my part that, in reading pages which this hand penned formerly, I often lose sight of the text under my eyes. It is not the words I see; but that past day; that bygone page of life's history; that tragedy, comedy it may be, which our little home company was enacting; that merry-making which we shared; that funeral which we followed; that bitter, bitter grief which we buried.

And, such being the state of my mind, I pray gentle readers to deal kindly with their humble servant's manifold shortcomings, blunders, and slips of memory. As sure as I read a page of my own composition, I find a fault or two, half a dozen. Jones is called Brown. Brown, who is dead, is brought to life. Aghast, and months after the number was printed, I saw that I had called Philip Firmin, Clive Newcome. Now Clive Newcome is the hero of another story by the reader's most obedient writer. The two men are as different, in my mind's eye, as – as Lord Palmerston and Mr

Disraeli let us say.[11] But there is that blunder at page 990, line 76, volume 84 of the *Cornhill Magazine*, and it is past mending; and I wish in my life I had made no worse blunders or errors than that which is hereby acknowledged.

Another Finis written. Another mile-stone passed on this journey from birth to the next world! Sure it is a subject for solemn cogitation. Shall we continue this story-telling business and be voluble to the end of our age? Will it not be presently time, O prattler, to hold your tongue, and let younger people speak? I have a friend, a painter, who, like other persons who shall be nameless, is growing old. He has never painted with such laborious finish as his works now show. This master is still the most humble and diligent of scholars.[12] Of Art, his mistress, he is always an eager, reverent pupil. In his calling, in yours, in mine, industry and humility will help and comfort us. A word with you. In a pretty large experience I have not found the men who write books superior in wit or learning to those who don't write at all. In regard of mere information, non-writers must often be superior to writers. You don't expect a lawyer in full practice to be conversant with all kinds of literature; he is too busy with his law; and so a writer is commonly too busy with his own books

11. Liberal and Conservative prime ministers.
12. Thackeray is, I think, referring to Daniel Maclise (1806–70) – his friend and Dickens's. Maclise did notable portraits of both authors and was thought excellent company.

to be able to bestow attention on the works of other people. After a day's work (in which I have been depicting, let us say, the agonies of Louisa on parting with the Captain, or the atrocious behaviour of the wicked Marquis to Lady Emily)[13] I march to the Club, proposing to improve my mind and keep myself 'posted up', as the Americans phrase it, with the literature of the day. And what happens? Given, a walk after luncheon, a pleasing book, and a most comfortable armchair by the fire, and you know the rest. A doze ensues. Pleasing book drops suddenly, is picked up once with an air of some confusion, is laid presently softly in lap: head falls on comfortable arm-chair cushion: eyes close: soft nasal music is heard. Am I telling Club secrets? Of afternoons, after lunch, I say, scores of sensible fogies have a doze. Perhaps I have fallen asleep over that very book to which 'Finis' has just been written. 'And if the writer sleeps, what happens to the readers?' says Jones, coming down upon me with his lightning wit. What? You *did* sleep over it? And a very good thing too. These eyes have more than once seen a friend dozing over pages which this hand has written. There is a vignette somewhere in one of my books of a friend so caught napping with 'Pendennis', or the 'Newcomes', in his lap and if a writer can give you a sweet soothing, harmless sleep, has he not done you a kindness? So is the author who excites and interests you worthy of

13. Plot details from *Philip*, published in the *Cornhill Magazine*, Jan 1861–August 1862, alongside Thackeray's Roundabouts.

your thanks and benedictions. I am troubled with fever and ague, that seizes me at odd intervals and prostrates me for a day.[14] There is cold fit, for which, I am thankful to say, hot brandy-and-water is prescribed, and this induces hot fit, and so on. In one or two of these fits I have read novels with the most fearful contentment of mind. Once, on the Mississippi, it was my dearly beloved 'Jacob Faithful': once at Frankfort O. M., the delightful 'Vingt Ans Après' of Monsieur Dumas: once at Tunbridge Wells, the thrilling 'Woman in White':[15] and these books gave me amusement from morning till sunset. I remember those ague fits with a great deal of pleasure and gratitude. Think of a whole day in bed, and a good novel for a companion! No cares: no remorse about idleness: no visitors: and the Woman in White or the Chevalier d'Artagnan to tell me stories from dawn to night! 'Please, ma'am, my master's compliments, and can he have the third volume?' (This message was sent to an astonished friend and neighbour who lent me, volume by volume, the W. in W.) How do you like your novels? I like mine strong, 'hot with', and no mistake: no love-making: no observations about society: little dialogue, except where the characters are bullying each other: plenty of fighting:

14. Thackeray's health was declining at this point of his life. He had urethral problems, was overweight, overworked, and would, in a few months, die of a stroke.
15. *Jacob Faithful; or, The Adventures of a Waterman* (1834) by (Captain) Frederick Marryat (1834); *Twenty Years After* (1845) by Alexandre Dumas; *The Woman in White* (1860) by Wilkie Collins.

and a villain in the cupboard, who is to suffer tortures just before Finis. I don't like your melancholy Finis. I never read the history of a consumptive heroine twice. If I might give a short hint to an impartial writer (as the *Examiner* used to say in old days), it would be to act, *not* à la mode le pays de Pole (I think that was the phraseology), but *always* to give quarter.[16] In the story of Philip, just come to an end, I have the permission of the author to state, that he was going to drown the two villains of the piece – a certain Doctor F –– and a certain Mr T. H.–– on board the 'President', or some other tragic ship – but you see I relented. I pictured to myself Firmin's ghastly face amid the crowd of shuddering people on that reeling deck in the lonely ocean, and thought, 'Thou ghastly lying wretch, thou shalt not be drowned: thou shalt have a fever only; a knowledge of thy danger; and a chance – ever so small a chance – of repentance.'[17] I wonder whether he *did* repent when he found himself in the yellow-fever, in Virginia? The probability is, he fancied that his son had injured him very much, and forgave him on his death-bed. Do you imagine there is a great deal of genuine right-down remorse in the world? Don't people rather find excuses which make their minds easy; endeavour to prove to themselves that they have been lamentably belied and

16. Not to act with Polish ruthlessness, but always to show mercy. It is found, obscurely, in the *Examiner* political weekly, 3 Dec 1837, advising the government how to form its new ministry.
17. Plot detail about Philip's irrepressibly roguish father.

misunderstood; and try and forgive the persecutors who *will* present that bill when it is due; and not bear malice against the cruel ruffian who takes them to the police-office for stealing them spoons? Years ago I had a quarrel with a certain well-known person (I believed a statement regarding him which his friends imparted to me, and which turned out to be quite incorrect). To his dying day that quarrel was never quite made up. I said to his brother, 'Why is your brother's soul still dark against me? It is I who ought to be angry and unforgiving: for I was in the wrong.' In the region which they now inhabit (for Finis has been set to the volumes of the lives of both here below), if they take any cognizance of our squabbles, and tittle-tattles, and gossips on earth here, I hope they admit that my little error was not of a nature unpardonable. If you have never committed a worse, my good sir, surely the score against you will not be heavy. Ha, *dilectissimi fratres*![18] It is in regard of sins *not* found out that we may say or sing (in an undertone, in a most penitent and lugubrious minor key), 'Miserere nobis miseris peccatoribus.'[19]

Among the sins of commission which novel-writers not seldom perpetrate, is the sin of grandiloquence, or tall-talking, against which, for my part, I will offer up a special *libera me*.[20] This is the sin of

18. Dearly beloved. Thackeray is sermonising, self-mockingly.
19. From the Latin Anglican liturgy. Lord have mercy upon us.
20. 'Deliver me'; Thackeray is getting very theological and is here borrowing from Catholic confession.

schoolmasters, governesses, critics, sermoners, and instructors of young or old people. Nay (for I am making a clean breast, and liberating my soul), perhaps of all the novel-spinners now extant, the present speaker is the most addicted to preaching. Does he not stop perpetually in his story and begin to preach to you? When he ought to be engaged with business, is he not for ever taking the Muse by the sleeve, and plaguing her with some of his cynical sermons? I cry *peccavi*[21] loudly and heartily. I tell you I would like to be able to write a story which should show no egotism whatever – in which there should be no reflections, no cynicism, no vulgarity (and so forth), but an incident in every other page, a villain, a battle, a mystery in every chapter. I should like to be able to feed a reader so spicily as to leave him hungering and thirsting for more at the end of every monthly meal.

Alexandre Dumas describes himself, when inventing the plan of a work, as lying silent on his back for two whole days on the deck of a yacht in a Mediterranean port. At the end of the two days he arose and called for dinner. In those two days he had built his plot. He had moulded a mighty clay, to be cast presently in perennial brass. The chapters, the characters, the incidents, the combinations were all arranged in the artist's brain ere he set a pen to paper. My Pegasus won't fly, so as to let me survey the field

21. I have sinned.

below me. He has no wings, he is blind of one eye certainly, he is restive, stubborn, slow; crops a hedge when he ought to be galloping, or gallops when he ought to be quiet. He never will show off when I want him. Sometimes he goes at a pace which surprises me. Sometimes, when I most wish him to make the running, the brute turns restive, and I am obliged to let him take his own time. I wonder do other novel-writers experience this fatalism? They *must* go a certain way, in spite of themselves. I have been surprised at the observations made by some of my characters. It seems as if an occult Power was moving the pen. The personage does or says something, and I ask, how the dickens did he come to think of that? Every man has remarked in dreams, the vast dramatic power which is sometimes evinced; I won't say the surprising power, for nothing does surprise you in dreams. But those strange characters you meet make instant observations of which you never can have thought previously. In like manner, the imagination foretells things. We spake anon of the inflated style of some writers. What also if there is an *afflated* style, – when a writer is like a Pythoness[22] on her oracle tripod, and mighty words, words which he cannot help, come blowing, and bellowing, and whistling, and moaning through the speaking pipes of his bodily organ? I have told you it was a very queer shock to me the other day when,

22. Female soothsayer. The Oracle of Delphi sat in a cauldron on a tripod.

with a letter of introduction in his hand, the artist's (not my) Philip Firmin walked into this room, and sat down in the chair opposite. In the novel of *Pendennis*, written ten years ago, there is an account of a certain Costigan, whom I had invented (as I suppose authors invent their personages out of scraps, heel-taps, odds and ends of characters). I was smoking in a tavern parlour one night – and this Costigan came into the room alive – the very man: – the most remarkable resemblance of the printed sketches of the man, of the rude drawings in which I had depicted him. He had the same little coat, the same battered hat, cocked on one eye, the same twinkle in that eye. 'Sir,' said I, knowing him to be an old friend whom I had met in unknown regions, 'Sir,' I said, 'may I offer you a glass of brandy-and-water?' *'Bedad, ye may,'* says he, *'and I'll sing ye a song tu.'* Of course he spoke with an Irish brogue. Of course he had been in the army. In ten minutes he pulled out an Army Agent's account, whereon his name was written. A few months after we read of him in a police court. How had I come to know him, to divine him? Nothing shall convince me that I have not seen that man in the world of spirits. In the world of spirits and water I know I did: but that is a mere quibble of words. I was not surprised when he spoke in an Irish brogue. I had had cognizance of him before somehow. Who has not felt that little shock which arises when a person, a place, some words in a book (there is always a collocation) present themselves to you, and you know that you have before met the same person, words, scene, and so forth?

They used to call the good Sir Walter the 'Wizard of the North'.[23] What if some writer should appear who can write so *enchantingly* that he shall be able to call into actual life the people whom he invents? What if Mignon, and Margaret, and Goetz von Berlichingen are alive now (though I don't say they are visible), and Dugald Dalgetty and Ivanhoe were to step in at that open window by the little garden yonder? Suppose Uncas and our noble old Leather Stocking were to glide silent in? Suppose Athos, Porthos, and Aramis should enter with a noiseless swagger, curling their moustaches? And dearest Amelia Booth, on Uncle Toby's arm; and Tittlebat Titmouse, with his hair dyed green; and all the Crummles company of comedians, with the Gil Blas troop; and Sir Roger de Coverley; and the greatest of all crazy gentlemen, the Knight of La Mancha, with his blessed squire?[24] I say to you, I look rather wistfully towards the window, musing upon these people. Were any of them to enter, I think I should not be very much frightened. Dear old friends,

23. Sir Walter Scott.
24. Uncas is the native American hero of *The Last of the Mohicans* by James Fenimore Cooper; Athos, etc, are the heroes in *The Three Musketeers* by Dumas; Amelia Booth is the heroine in Fielding's *Amelia*; Uncle Toby features in Sterne's *Tristram Shandy*; Gil Blas is the hero in the picaresque novel by Le Sage; Tittlebat Titmouse is the hero of Samuel Warren's *Ten Thousand a Year*; Sir Roger de Coverley is the letter writer created by Joseph Addison; and finally Thackeray's beloved Don Quixote.

what pleasant hours I have had with them! We do not see each other very often, but when we do, we are ever happy to meet. I had a capital half-hour with Jacob Faithful[25] last night; when the last sheet was corrected, when 'Finis' had been written, and the printer's boy, with the copy, was safe in Green Arbour Court.

So you are gone, little printer's boy, with the last scratches and corrections on the proof, and a fine flourish by way of Finis at the story's end. The last corrections? I say those last corrections seem never to be finished. A plague upon the weeds! Every day, when I walk in my own little literary garden-plot, I spy some, and should like to have a spud, and root them out. Those idle words, neighbour, are past remedy. That turning back to the old pages produces anything but elation of mind. Would you not pay a pretty fine to be able to cancel some of them? Oh, the sad old pages, the dull old pages! Oh, the cares, the *ennui*, the squabbles, the repetitions, the old conversations over and over again! But now and again a kind thought is recalled, and now and again a dear memory. Yet a few chapters more, and then the last: after which, behold Finis itself come to an end, and the Infinite begun.

25. Jacob Faithful is the hero of the novel of the same name by Captain Marryat.

Other titles from Notting Hill Editions*

On Christmas: A Seasonal Anthology
Introduced by Gyles Brandreth

This delightful anthology offers an array of writers old and
new who have expressed their thoughts about Christmas with
joy, nostalgia, grumpiness and wit. Includes selections from
Dickens, Dostoevsky, Thackeray, P. G. Wodehouse, Ali Smith,
Will Self and Queen Victoria.

The Paradoxal Compass: Drake's Dilemma
by Horatio Morpurgo

Both historical narrative and environmental manifesto,
Morpurgo dramatizes the perilous hours during which
Drake's *Golden Hinde* was stranded off the coast of Indonesia.
Morpurgo explores our complex relationship to the sea since
the Age of Discovery.

'A perfectly-formed treasure of a book' – Philip Hoare

Smoke
by John Berger & Selçuk Demirel

John Berger, art critic, novelist and long-time smoker, joins
forces with Turkish writer and illustrator Selçuk Demirel. This
charming pictorial essay reflects on the cultural implications of
smoking through a series of brilliantly inventive illustrations.

A Garden from a Hundred Packets of Seed
by James Fenton

In this light-hearted essay, poet and gardener James Fenton
describes a hundred plants he would choose to grow from seed.
Here is a happy, stylish, thought-provoking exercise in good
principles.

'A small book, yes, but how it grows in your mind after you
put it down.' – Jamaica Kincaid

You and Me: The Neuroscience of Identity
by Susan Greenfield

A fascinating look at the relationship between identity and
neuroscience in the age of social media. Greenfield looks at the
ways in which technology impacts our brains and sense
of identity.

Nairn's Towns
by Ian Nairn, Introduced by Owen Hatherley

Sixteen short essays on Northern cities and towns in Britain.
Ian Nairn (1930–1983) coined the term 'Subtopia' for the areas
around cities that had been failed by urban planning. His work
has influenced writers such as Will Self and Iain Sinclair.

'Once you discover Nairn you want to read everything
he's written.' – *Daily Telegraph*

CLASSIC COLLECTION

The Classic Collection brings together the finest essayists of the past, introduced by contemporary writers.

The Russian Soul
– Selections from A Writer's Diary by Fyodor Dostoevsky
Introduced by Rosamund Bartlett

Drawn from Life – Selected Essays of Michel de Montaigne
Introduced by Tim Parks

Grumbling at Large – Selected Essays of J. B. Priestley
Introduced by Valerie Grove

Beautiful and Impossible Things
– Selected Essays of Oscar Wilde
Introduced by Gyles Brandreth

Words of Fire – Selected Essays of Ahad Ha'am
Introduced by Brian Klug

Essays on the Self – Selected Essays of Virginia Woolf
Introduced by Joanna Kavenna

All That is Worth Remembering
– Selected Essays of William Hazlitt
Introduced by Duncan Wu

*All NHE titles are available in the UK, and some titles are available in the rest of the world. For more information, please visit www.nottinghilleditions.com.

A selection of our titles is distributed in the US and Canada by New York Review Books. For more information on available titles, please visit www.nyrb.com.